The ULTIMATE
New-Home Buying Guide

Insiders Reveal the Secrets
Builders Don't Want You to Know

The ULTIMATE
New-Home Buying Guide

Insiders Reveal the Secrets
Builders Don't Want You to Know

Jeff and Susan
Treganowan

Maple Leaf Press

www.MapleLeafPress.com

Note: This publication contains the opinion of the authors. The authors have made every attempt to present accurate information at the time of publication. This book is meant to assist the reader in the process of purchasing a new home. The publisher and the authors assume no responsibility for errors and omissions. It is not intended to provide legal or engineering information. In all legal matters the reader should consult with a competent real estate attorney.

The publisher and authors specifically disclaim any responsibility for any liability, loss or risk, personal or otherwise, which is incurred as a result, directly or indirectly, of the use and application of any of the contents of this book.

The Ultimate New-Home Buying Guide may be purchased for business or promotions at a reduced bulk rate price. Please write to the Market Director, Maple Leaf Press, P.O. Box 5002-115, No. Conway, NH 03860-5002. You may also send e-mail to Mktdir@MapleLeafPress.com.

Printed in the United States of America

ISBN 0-9706737-0-1

Library of Congress Card Number: 00-193216

Publisher's Cataloging-in-Publication
(Provided by Quality Books, Inc.)

Treganowan, Jeff
    The ultimate new home buying guide: insiders reveal the secrets builders don't want you to know / Jeff and Susan Treganowan. – 1st ed.
    p. cm.
    Includes index.
    LCCN: 00-193216
    ISBN: 0-9706737-0-1

    1. House buying. 2. Residential real estate-Purchasing. 3. House construction. I. Treganowan, Susan. II. Title.

TH4817.5.T74 2001   643'.12
                                                 QBI00-1057

Dear New-Home Buyer,

Congratulations! You have taken the first step in taking control of buying your new home, by picking up our book. This book will guide you through the home-buying process from start to finish. Imagine having a very good friend on the inside of the new-home building industry, because that is exactly what you are holding in your hands. Builders cannot take advantage of Insiders because they know every secret they try to hide. You are now going to become an Insider.

Jeff and I have been new-home agents for several years. We have had the pleasure of working with thousands of new-home buyers just like you. Some of our most enjoyable moments have been handing out keys to excited couples moving into their new home. The joy we have seen in happy homeowners' faces has warmed our hearts over and over again.

Unfortunately, we have had the terrible experience of seeing hundreds of disappointed faces as well. The stress and frustration would come from delays, poor construction, and broken promises made by the builder. We have seen many new-home buyers taken advantage of and overcharged for features in their homes. But even worse, we have seen builders perform shoddy construction in a rush to meet deadlines. We're not going to let this happen to you.

We want to add you to our growing list of happy homeowners. By reading *The Ultimate New-Home Buying Guide,* your new-home experience will be fun, exciting, and as stress-free as possible. We are eager to hear how you took control and had a wonderful adventure buying your new home. Won't you join our happy group of Insiders by writing and sharing your experience with us soon?

Susan and Jeff Treganowan
c/o Maple Leaf Press
P.O. Box 5002-115
North Conway, NH 03860-5002
E-mail: Author@MapleLeafPress.com

What People Are Saying about the The Ultimate New-Home Buying Guide

"This book is **ABSOLUTELY NECESSARY** *if you want a quality-built new home. Read it and you will become a happy home-buyer instead of a distressed homeowner."*

—HADD (Homeowners Against Deficient Dwellings),
www.hadd.com

"This book is a necessary and helpful tool for all new-home buyers. Jeff and Susan's knowledge of the real estate industry and their genuine care and concern for their buyers yield this **MUST HAVE** *guide to purchasing a new home."*

—Claudine Branchaud, senior loan officer

"This TELL-ALL book takes the mystery out of buying a new home and puts power in the hands of the buyers. The process can be stressful, which is why this book is such a great tool. Knowledge can be a great leveler."

—Barbara Rigali, retired new-home agent

About the Authors

Jeff and Susan Treganowan are new-home experts who have had great success selling new homes in Las Vegas, Nevada, for many years. Together they have worked for several new-home builders not only in sales but also in developing marketing programs. The authors have always fought for honest marketing practices and quality construction in the new-home industry. When they were forced to either adopt a completely dishonest marketing program from a builder or take early retirement, the authors opted for retirement. "We simply refused to lie to our buyers."

The Ultimate New-Home Buying Guide exposes dishonest practices that many builders use. The authors have researched builders from coast to coast and discovered the same methods are used throughout the country. Jeff is very experienced in exposing wrongdoing as he has a long history of being a whistle-blower.

In 1982 Jeff exposed an Air Force discrimination policy that was directed against women. **Senator Ted Kennedy** and **Congressman Barney Frank** supported him in saving a woman's job and getting the Air Force policy eliminated.

In 1991 Jeff went to the **United States Congress** again to stop the military from sending troops into the **Gulf War** with gas mask inserts that were fitted incorrectly. After a worldwide interview on **CNN,** a congressional order was given to the military to stop using the inferior masks.

Now Jeff and Susan are on a national campaign to get a **Homebuyer's Protection Addendum (HPA)** adopted. They simply want home builders to guarantee a quality home delivered on time, with everything in the house complete. The authors are donating 10% of their earnings from this book to *(HADD) Homeowners Against Deficient Dwellings* (www.hadd.com). This national consumer group fights for new-home buyers' rights.

Table of Contents

Would you move into this home? It did not pass city inspection or have an FHA appraisal, but the builder still considered the home in "acceptable condition to close" and it did. Read this book, and don't let this happen to you!!

Introduction

Did the picture on the previous page shock you? I hope it did. I was the unfortunate agent who had to deliver that new home. As new-home agents, Susan and I have worked for several builders in the Las Vegas and Henderson areas of Nevada. We have learned how builders make their money and how they manipulate buyers. This book reveals the builder's secrets to give you the advantage when buying a new home. This book will make you an Insider.

If you are even thinking about buying a new home, this book is for you. If you are looking at resales that are less than five years old, then this book will show you how to do research to find the good builders, so you will get a well-constructed home. We have searched bookstores across the country for a complete guide that tells the real story about buying new homes. We found nothing specifically for you, the new-home buyer, so we decided it was time there was a guide for the buyer. Of the different books out there, ours is the only book actually written by new-home agents, so it's the only one that can give you the true inside story. Although other books guess at what you might be able to do, we use our experience to tell you exactly what you can and must do. And you come away as an Insider because of this information.

First-Time Buyers: If this will be your first new home, then this book will become your bible. This book will teach you everything that you must know about finding a new home, getting a loan, getting big savings and a quality built home. *The Ultimate New-Home Buying Guide* will take you from novice to expert.

Experienced Buyers: If you are an experienced buyer, then this book will give you your PhD. You will learn Insider information in this book that can save you thousands of dollars on the price of the home and upgrades. You will also learn proven techniques to ensure that your home is built with quality.

Realtors: Learn Insider techniques to save your clients money. Learn how Insiders research a builder and make sure your clients get a quality built home. With the Insider information in this book, you will truly be a new-home specialist.

Did you know that builders use several techniques to control the unsuspecting buyer? For example, the contracts are written for the benefit of the builders, and they are protected if they fail to deliver your house on time, even if it is 6 months late! Did you also know that the builders plan on moving you into your home before it is finished? Take a second look at the home on the opening page. The builder's goal is to control the buyer every step of the way, from the model home tour through the construction phase, and finally the closing. And it is the responsibility of the new-home agent to keep and maintain control throughout the whole process.

Now, we have the good news. Susan and I are going to become your personal expert advisors. We are going to guide you every step of the way so that you can gain control from the start. This is not a book to give you general ideas of what you might be able to do. This is a complete step-by-step guide on finding the right home, the right builder, and the best price. There will be pictures or real-life examples in each chapter so that you can understand real-world scenarios. We can show you these proven techniques and more because of our experience with builders, and we know what makes them perform.

You can save thousands of dollars by learning how to negotiate. Imagine yourself negotiating to buy a new car. Now imagine if you knew what the dealer's profit was and what options he can give away to make a deal. With this Insider information, you would be able to make a fabulous deal. This book will give you the same Insider's position when negotiating the price and terms of your new home. The negotiation process in purchasing a new home is a game of knowledge and skill; if you lack either of these qualities, then you will be at a great disadvantage and lose every time. But Insiders know how to determine the builder's profit as it changes in different situations. We will share our knowledge and teach you our skills, so that you will become an Insider.

We should mention that we use the pronouns *he* or *she* throughout this book for simplicity only. We are in no way suggesting that gender should be a consideration in any of the professions that we discuss. We have worked with men and women as new-home agents, loan officers, superintendents, department heads, and builders. In some examples, we will actually give a name to certain positions to add realism to the example. These names are purely fictional, and they are used only to clarify the examples that we use.

Well, let's get started on our journey. Remember, we are going to cover everything you need to know to find and purchase your new home. The chapters are set up in chronological order. We start with deciding what kind of home you want or need, and we finish with moving into your new home. We highly recommend that you read every chapter in order. The information that you learn in each chapter will prepare you for the next. There will be tables, pictures, and questions in some of the chapters to help clarify each step that we take.

After you have finished the whole book, you will be ready to start your new-home search as an Insider. You can refer to any chapter as often as you like. You can use the techniques in this book over and over again. We want you to be a confident, astute buyer when you enter your first model home because the model home is their home turf. Don't worry: We'll be with you every step of the way. At the end of our journey together, you will be the proud bearer of a new title; you will be an Insider!

Chapter 1

What Kind of House Do You Want or Need?

In this chapter:

- The Advantages and Disadvantages of Owning Your Own Home
- The Difference between Condos, Townhouses, and Single-Family Homes
- The Difference between Custom, Semi-Custom, and Production Homes
- The Benefits and Problems with Homeowner's Associations (HOAs)
- The Importance of Resale Value
- Deciding What Features You Want in Your Home
- Chapter Summary

If this will be your first home, or even your second or fifth, you can spend hours and hours thinking about what you want in a home. How many bedrooms? What size should the garage be? Do you want a two-story or a one-story home? How big should your kitchen be? Do you really need a family room and a living room? In today's new-home market, you can find just about anything that you want. It's fine to get what you want, but many people have trouble separating their *wants* from their *needs*. A *want* is something that you believe will be fun to have in a home, such as an entertainment room with a full wet bar. A *need* is that third or fourth bedroom to accommodate your child with a place to sleep. Although we don't pretend to know what your personal desires are, this chapter will give you some ideas to help you pick out features in a home that will satisfy both your *wants* and *needs*. We are also going to discuss the upgrades that will increase the resale value of your home. Some structural upgrades will increase the resale value; most upgrades will only make the house more salable. The different features in your home will vary according to what type of home you buy. It might also be possible that in your current situation you are better off renting instead of buying. So we will start this chapter by explaining the difference between renting and owning.

The Advantages and Disadvantages of Owning Your Own Home

Advantages

When you own your own home, you have the right to do what you want with it. You can paint the walls, change the flooring, or even change the building structure if you own a single-family home. Obviously, you cannot do all of that when you are renting. When you own, it is *your place,* and you have the freedom to change it in any way you like. It is a great feeling to say, "I own it," and in the financial world it can add respect. When you apply for different types of financing in the future, you will be considered a better risk if you are a homeowner rather than a renter. Eventually, you will even be able to borrow money against the equity that you have built up in your home.

Owning your own home not only provides you with a place to live, but it is an investment as well. As you pay off your mortgage, you owe less on your home and, at the same time, the value of your home should be appreciating. With few exceptions, the value of a home will go up every year, but the amount of that appreciation can vary drastically across the country. We suggest that you talk to your local real estate professionals for an estimate of the appreciation for your area. Equity in your home is determined by how much of the mortgage you have paid off, plus how much the value of your property has appreciated. For example, if you have paid off $20,000 of your mortgage loan and the value of the home has appreciated by $10,000, then your total equity in the home would be $30,000. If you then sold your home for the appraised value, you would receive $30,000 after your mortgage was paid, less any Realtor and closing costs. Although homes usually do appreciate, it is also possible to have homes lose their value. One of the chief reasons that will cause homes to depreciate or lose their value is due to their location, which we will discuss in detail in chapter 3.

Everyone hates paying taxes, and you get a big tax break when you own a home. When you make your mortgage payments for your home, the interest portion of your payment is tax deductible. This can make a big difference at the end of the year when you file your income tax return. If you are renting, you might be making the same payment to a landlord, but the landlord gets the tax break instead of you.

One final advantage to owning your own home is having fixed housing costs. A landlord can raise your rent every year if he or she desires to do so. As long as you have a fixed interest rate home mortgage, your monthly payment will never go up.

Disadvantages

When you get a leak in one of your sinks, guess who gets to fix it? With a single-family home, there will usually be a yard with grass to mow and plants to trim and water. You may want to watch the big football game or take a day trip in the car, but your front yard is starting to look like a wild field of grass. Usually, the neighbors will be very interested in your wild field of grass if it does not get mowed. Mowing the lawn and trimming the plants might take precedence over being able to watch that football game or taking that day trip. Taking care of a home demands a lot more of your time than living in an apartment. You must be willing to take that time because house maintenance must be done regularly to avoid costly repairs and unhappy relationships with your neighbors. When you own a home, there is one thing that never changes: There is always something that needs to be done.

If you work for a company that requires you to move every two or three years, then owning may not be the best decision. It is hard to pay the selling costs and not lose money on a home when you have lived there for only two or three years. When you own a house, you usually have to sell it before you can leave the area. If you are trying to sell a house in a bad neighborhood, we have seen it take years. It is much easier to move to a new location when you are renting.

Most people who have a choice would rather own than rent. The financial benefits and personal satisfaction of gaining the "American Dream" usually far outweigh the freedom of fewer responsibilities associated with renting. Let us now discuss some different types of houses available.

The Difference between Condos, Townhouses, and Single-Family Homes

Condos (Condominiums)

You can think of a condo, sometimes called *co-op,* basically as an apartment that you own. People who are drawn to condos are trying to get the benefits of both renting an apartment and owning a new home. Condos are usually less expensive than single-family homes because you are not getting any private land with the sale; the homeowners communally own the land that the condo buildings sit on. Because you are not getting any private land, your property taxes will be less than a single-family home. If cost is a barrier to buying, then a condo might be an option to own and still get the mortgage tax break. Condos generally come with all maintenance of the common grounds performed by the homeowner's association (HOA). This might include landscaped areas, a clubhouse, or even a pool. For a person who does not want to take the time to maintain a home (*and watch the football game instead*), a condo might be the right choice. Because there are no grounds to maintain, the only maintenance required is inside the unit. The other side of the coin is that there is no private yard where your children can play. You will not have a private area outside to just sit and read a wonderful book, such as the one you are reading right now. Families with children will find living in a condo much the same as living in an apartment.

Because condo owners share common walls, it can be confusing at times to determine who has the responsibility for repairing certain problems that occur. One owner we know who lived in a downstairs condo had his home flooded when a woman upstairs let her tub run over for several hours. The condo association's insurance did not cover anything in this situation because a communal wall did not cause the damage. The owner of the upstairs condo caused the damage; her homeowner's insurance paid for damages inside her condo, but nothing outside of it. The downstairs homeowner had to go to court to get his damages repaired by the upstairs homeowner. Typically, the condo association insurance covers only "communal" property. Be aware: You can be affected by your neighbors' accidents when they damage more than just their own homes. The moral of the story—If you do decide to buy a condo, it is imperative that you know exactly what your condo policy covers and what additional insurance you will need to purchase.

Townhouses

Townhouses are similar in maintenance to a condo or co-op with the exception of having small private yards in some communities. Townhouses often have garages attached to the unit and offer a bit more privacy than a condo. It is essentially like taking one step toward having a single-family home. Townhouses can offer more privacy and more square footage in the home, but you will still have connecting walls and the strict homeowner's association (HOA). HOAs are always more expensive and more strict in a condo or townhouse community. Depending upon the maintenance requirements, we have seen monthly HOA dues run into the hundreds of dollars. In most condo or townhouse communities, the association dues can rise by 10% a year without a majority vote of the homeowners approving it. You should know that HOA dues are higher when there is a pool, weight room, or something like a community room. Not only does the HOA pay to maintain these amenities and common areas, but they pay for the expensive liability insurance to cover them, too. This may be acceptable if you are taking advantage of all the amenities offered, but it has been our experience that most people in these living arrangements pay for a lot more than they use.

One despicable practice that we have seen some builders use is to advertise very low association dues when selling the community. The builder pays the HOA dues for unsold units. Typically, the builder's landscaping contract or construction crew maintain the neighborhood common areas, thus keeping the HOA costs low while the neighborhood is being built. This looks attractive to buyers, but after the community is sold out, the homeowners discover the brutal financial truth: The monthly dues will not support the community. We have seen dues almost double within months after the builder has sold out the community, when all the maintenance costs fell upon the homeowner's association's shoulders. If you are looking at a co-op community with a lot of amenities and very low monthly dues, we recommend being very cautious. In chapter 7, you will learn how to do research so you won't have this problem; for now, just know that it exists.

A good rule of thumb when thinking about a condo or townhouse is to think of it as buying an apartment. For example, you will hear your neighbor's music just as clearly in a condo as you will in an apartment. We will talk about resale value later in this chapter, but generally it will be much lower with a condo or a townhouse than it will be with a single-family home.

Single-Family Homes

Single-family homes are detached dwellings that sit on their own piece of real estate. These homes may be on a small lot or be sitting on several acres of land. The main point is that they do sit on their own land. If you want privacy, then you want a single-family home.

In many of the newer home communities, you will have a homeowner's association (HOA), but the dues will be much less than in a condo or a townhouse. This is because there are no common grounds to maintain. There are exceptions, for example, if you live in a Master-planned Community (master plan). Some master plans have common grounds, clubhouses, playgrounds, pools, and more. Even with these amenities, the dues usually are still far lower than co-op communities because you have more people to help pay them.

Single-family homes are what most people desire to have. Most people who become homeowners want space—room for their children to play, to have a barbecue on their patios, or they need a yard for their pets. Single-family homes almost always will appreciate faster in value than co-ops; it is simply a matter of greater demand. When buying a new single-family home, you can go three ways: custom, semi-custom, and production homes.

The Difference between Custom, Semi-Custom, and Production Homes

Custom Homes

When building a custom home, you hire an architect to design your home, and you have complete control over the materials that you put into your home. Unless you are a general contractor, you will need to hire one. The general contractor will hire and oversee the construction performed by subcontractors. The subcontractors will be the framers, plumbers, electricians, and so forth. Everything from doorstops and floorboards to roof tiles—essentially the level of quality materials that go into the house—will be up to you. If you do not know about "building grade materials" and "quality materials," you had better learn before starting a building project. It is not uncommon to have a homeowner be charged for quality materials when lower building grade materials were used.

If you decide to custom build, make sure you get as many references about your general contractor as you can. The complete building of your new custom home is going to rest in this person's hands. We recommend following the "Rule of Three" and interview at least three general contractors before deciding whom to hire. This type of building will require you to be knowledgeable in the construction field, or you will have to completely trust the contractor that you hire. If you do intend to custom build your home, there are books that discuss custom building in great detail. All of the techniques in this book do apply to custom building, and you need to have this information. However, custom building requires more detail and technical building knowledge that you must have before you build. We recommend going to your library or bookstore and researching custom building in detail. When it comes to minimizing cost overruns, sticking to your budget, and getting a quality built home—you just cannot depend on the general contractor. You need to depend on yourself. We don't know of a single person who custom built their home that stayed at or under budget, and who wasn't intimately involved in the actual construction of their home.

According to the National Association of Home Builders, only 8% of all new homes will be custom built. This book was written mainly to address the 92% who will be buying semi-custom and production new homes, which we will move to now.

Semi-Custom Homes

Semi-custom homes are available to meet almost every person's wants and needs in today's new-home market. Would you like to have several options to design your house without the uncertainty of hiring a general contractor? Then the semi-custom home market is your choice today. We have sold semi-custom homes that have had hundreds of unique upgrades such as elevators and carriage houses. Today, semi-custom builders will change almost everything in a floor plan with the exception of load-bearing walls. Load-bearing walls must stay in place to support the weight of the roof, ceiling, and upper floors of the house. When looking at a semi-custom home, the buyer will have pages of options and upgrades from which to choose. Generally, a semi-custom community will have from three to ten floor-plan choices. From there, the buyer may make changes in room sizes, the amount of rooms, and maybe even reorganize rooms. The list of upgrades in most cases is endless. Often the builders will accept special option ideas you bring to them called a *nonstandard change*—a change not on their options lists.

In any city where there are a lot of new-home builders, there will also be a good number of semi-custom builders. You will still research the builders for the best one, and we explain this in more detail in chapter 7. However, unless you want to design and choose every little thing personally, almost everyone can find the home of his or her dreams in the semi-custom home market. One of the biggest advantages with a semi-custom home is that there are no cost overruns. You know the exact price before the building starts, and it will not change.

Production Homes

Production homes are what many people call *tract homes*. Usually, they will have three or four floor-plan choices, and they will offer a limited selection of options and upgrades. Structural changes will also be limited because it slows down production. Production homes are the least expensive of the three types of new homes. They key word is *production*. Production communities need to build as many homes as possible and as quickly as possible. That is why upgrades and structural changes are limited. Every time a builder makes a nonstandard change, it slows down the construction process. This costs the builder more money and in turn raises the price of the house. This does not mean that you cannot get a high-quality production home.

What many people do not realize is that many of the same sub-contractors who work on a production community drive down the street to do the same work on semi-custom and custom homes. Just how good that subcontractor will be on either of these jobs depends on the superintendent at the job site. Many of the larger builders in the country build production, semi-custom, and custom homes. For the most part, the same subcontractors will work on all three communities. The superintendent is the most influential person who will make the difference between quality construction and poor construction. There have been several cases where a subcontractor who has done excellent work on a production home has also done very poor work on a semi-custom or custom home. There can be several reasons for these varying degrees of competency, which we will cover extensively in chapter 7. For now, please realize that paying more for a house does not guarantee better construction.

The Benefits and Problems with Homeowner's Associations (HOAs)

HOAs are associations that are formed to preserve the value of a community. The theory behind these associations is that if certain rules are enforced, they will maintain the quality of life in the community, and your property value will continue to appreciate. Most new-home communities will have HOAs. We have seen associations that are very basic and seem to have logical rules. For example, homeowners are not allowed to have cars that are up on blocks parked in front of their houses. This would take away from the streetscape of the neighborhood. Boats and motor homes are generally not allowed to be parked in front of the house. Again, these rules make sense to preserve the appearance of the neighborhood.

Most people have no problems with HOAs as long as they keep within simple, logical boundaries. In fact, HOAs do serve a purpose and do help a community preserve a good quality of life in most cases. Associations that get out of hand are the ones that cause homeowners a lot of grief. Some HOAs, especially in the case of condos or townhouses, are so restrictive that they can make a homeowner wonder if he owns anything at all. In one Master-planned Community, they actually had "garage police." Security staff from the association would drive the community to make sure that no one left their garage door open. If you happened to leave your garage door open, you would usually be given a warning for the first offense. The second offense would get you a citation, and if it happened again, you would be fined $50.00. Does this sound oppressive? It may seem hard to believe that rules like these exist, but many do, and some people may want a really strict HOA. The point here is simple: Before you buy a home anywhere, you must read and understand the neighborhood HOA rules.

You must also read the covenants, conditions, and restrictions (CC&Rs). The CC&Rs are rules set up by the builder and/or county, which must be obeyed the same as any law. They will cover any health regulations, like how many animals you may have in your yard, and they may also contain restrictions on building additions onto your house. The CC&R and HOA documents must be read and understood before you sign any contract for a house. Don't let any Realtor or new-home agent tell you that there is nothing special in the association's rules or the CC&Rs. Most new-home agents have probably never read these documents, let alone know the neighborhood rules that you would have to obey. Remember, it's not the agent's responsibility to know the CC&R and HOA rules; it is yours. Knowing the rules before you buy will make sure that they fit into your lifestyle.

The Importance of Resale Value

It cannot be said enough, and you have heard it before: The three most important rules in real estate are location, location, and location. When you buy a new home, you are concerned with the neighborhood, location of schools, and shopping, among other things. Having these amenities close by and being in a convenient location adds value to your house. When you are looking for a new home, you should not have any reservations about the location of the community. You will see some great deals on houses that are located in less than desirable neighborhoods. You must remember that if you have any hesitation about buying that home, then someone will have the same hesitation when you want to sell it. We would never advise anyone to buy a new home in a marginal or poor location. If you have any doubts after driving through the neighborhood, and we suggest you drive through it at night as well as the day, then do not buy. It is our experience that neighborhoods deteriorate more often than they improve. If you purchase a home in a marginal area, there is a good chance that the neighborhood will turn into a bad area by the time you attempt to sell it. You could actually get stuck losing money. That "great deal" you got has now turned into a money trap you can't afford to sell.

There are certain features in a home that can add to the resale value and some that detract from future sales. For example, many new homes offer an office option instead of one of the bedrooms. This room shows great in the models, but it detracts from the resale value. Most people who buy new homes have families, and they need bedrooms for their children. If you build an office in place of a bedroom, then that is what it must always be—an office, with no clothes closet and most likely a complete wall taken up with a double door entry. On the other hand, it is easy to set up an office in a bedroom using the closet for storage. Then, when you sell your home, you have another bedroom and closet to offer—more resale value.

Almost all options and upgrades that you install in your house will *not* improve the resale value of your home. Does this come as a shock? Many homeowners learn this the hard way when they sell their homes and find out that their beautiful granite countertops did not increase the value or purchase price of their home, nor do items such as upgraded carpet or a Jacuzzi tub. They will make your house more salable by getting people interested in it, but they don't increase its value. Salable means that your house will show better and make it easier to sell, but please understand that most upgrades will not increase the value of your house. There are a few exceptions—if you add bathrooms, bedrooms, or increase your garage size. These are considered structural options, and most structural options will increase the resale value. Resale value is determined by the appraisal of your home, which gives you your selling price. Basically, everyone has countertops; there is no credit given for more expensive material, but not everyone has a third bathroom. Table 1.1, "Where Features Make Their Contribution," will give you an idea of what we mean. It gives you a list of features you could have in your home and the effect they would have when you are ready to sell your home.

A good rule to remember is that the only reason to buy any option is to increase the quality of life for your family while you live there. You won't get an increase in resale value unless the upgrades are structural, such as that extra bathroom. You must take this into consideration when deciding how long you will own your home. If you plan on being there for only five or six years,

Table 1.1 Where Features Make Their Contribution

	Resale Value	More Salable
Tile floors		X
Fancy stair rails		X
Extra garage	X	
Covered porch	X	
Ceiling fans		X
Glass front door		X
Extra bedroom	X	
Fireplace	X	
Basement	X	
Extra phone lines		X
Granite countertops		X
Gold faucet fixtures		X
Backyard landscaping	X	
Extra bathroom	X	

then putting a lot of money into decorative options may not be worth the limited pleasure that you will receive in return. But if this is your dream house for life, then you may want to customize it completely. Your decision will also depend on how many options you get for free or for a very low cost. We will explore the art of negotiating for options extensively in chapter 8. Now that you know the difference between resale value and salability, let's talk about deciding what options and features you want to have in your home.

Deciding What Features You Want in Your Home

We have sold homes that have offered as little as two pages of upgrades per home to as many as sixty pages of upgrades that included several structural changes. Semi-custom homes and production homes have come a long way in the past five years. You will ultimately decide what you want in your home, but we want you to consider a few important factors first. How long will you live in your home? This will help you determine how many options you should purchase. It will also help you determine how many bedrooms you will need. You may have only one child now, but are you planning more? Even if you have no children and do not plan on having any, you should never buy a home with fewer than three bedrooms. When you go to sell your home, remember that the largest market will be families, and most will require at least three bedrooms. You should always have at least two full bathrooms for the same reason. Garages have become popular over the past few years with our booming economy. Many people have bought a lot of "toys" that they keep in their garages these days. If you can get a three-car garage, you will always get a better resale price for your home than if you have a two-car garage. Of course, we never recommend buying a one-car garage.

Before you visit your first model home, you should decide some very important criteria for what your home must have. For example, how many bedrooms and bathrooms do you want? How much square footage do you think you will need? Then, make a list of features that you want in your home. See Table 1.2, "Sample Wish List," for a suggested format. The features on the list may change many times as you see more models, but it will give you a starting point and send you in the right direction. While making your list, rank those features by their importance to you. As you visit the model homes, you can mark your list for what each model includes or offers as an option.

Table 1.2 shows how your wish list might look before you enter any model home. We've decided for this sample that we want to buy a two-story home with 3 bedrooms, 2 baths, and a 2-car garge, and we need about 1,400 square feet (sq. ft.). We may look at several different types of models, but we still will only document on our list the kind of home that we want. There is no sense tracking homes that don't fit our criteria of needs or wants. Table 1.3 shows you what the list might look like after visiting a few neighborhoods.

This listing format gives you the chance "at a glance" to compare which house fits your needs and wants the best. Notice how the most expensive house (Ivy Trellis Model #3) has more included features, and the least expensive house (Rose Garden Model #1) has the most options. You could end up paying as much, or more, if you bought the Rose Garden home and included all the options than you would have paid if you bought the standard Ivy Trellis home.

Table 1.2   Sample Wish List

Two-story; 3 beds; 2 baths; 2-car garage with at least 1,400 sq. ft.

Neighborhood: **Model #:**	Model #	Model #	Model #	Model #
Base Price				
Sq. Ft.				

Have to Have

M. bedroom—
   big closet
M. bath—
   separate shower/tub
Spindle-style stair rail
Granite countertops
Maple wood cabinets
Tiled front entryway
Space for office
Separate laundry room

Like to Have

3-car garage
Fireplace
Formal dining room
Kitchen island
Washtub in laundry
Linen closet
View
Glass front door
Ceiling fan
   in bedrooms
Cable outlet
   in bedrooms
Landscaped backyard
Front picture window

Table 1.3   Completed Sample Wish List

Two-story; 3 beds; 2 baths; 2-car garage with at least 1,400 sq. ft.

Neighborhood Model #:	Blue Bird Model #3	Valley Side Model #1	Rose Garden Model #1	Ivy Trellis Model #3
Base Price	**$125,000**	**$127,000**	**$115,000**	**$138,000**
Sq. Ft.	**1,435 sq. ft.**	**1,437 sq. ft.**	**1,395 sq. ft.**	**1,428 sq. ft.**
Have to Have				
M. bedroom—				
big closet	$$$	$$$	$$$	stand
M. bath—				
separate shower/tub	stand	stand	no	stand
Spindle-style				
stair rail	$$$	$$$	$$$	$$$
Granite countertops	$$$	stand	$$$	stand
Maple wood cabinets	$$$	$$$	$$$	$$$
Tiled front				
entryway	stand	stand	$$$	stand
Space for office	use F-dining	use F-dining	no	use 4th bed
Separate				
laundry room	no	stand	no	stand
Like to Have				
3-car garage	$$$	$$$	no	stand
Fireplace	$$$	$$$	$$$	stand
Formal				
dining room	stand	stand	no	stand
Kitchen island	no	$$$	$$$	$$$
Washtub				
in laundry	no	no	no	stand
Linen closet	stand	stand	$$$	stand
View	$$$	no	$$$	no
Glass front door	no	$$$	$$$	$$$
Ceiling fan				
in bedrooms	$$$	$$$	$$$	$$$
Cable outlet				
in bedrooms	stand	stand	stand	stand
Landscaped backyard	no	$$$	no	no
Front picture window	stand	no	no	$$$

KEY: Stand = included in the base price of the house
     $$$ = available as an option; you should list the cost
     No = not included in the base price and not available as an option
     M. bed or M. bath = Master bedroom or Master bathroom
     F-dining = formal dining room

You may have to compromise on your list of features when making your final decision on a home. This completed list will help make your decision easier. You may also have to base your decision on how much your home will cost you. In the next chapter, we will figure out how to pay for what you want.

Chapter Summary

We started this chapter by discussing some of the advantages and disadvantages of owning your own home, such as the tax breaks. We also talked about the secure, proud feeling of owning your own home.

We discussed the differences between condos, townhouses, and single-family homes. You learned that owning a condo or townhouse would be very similar to owning an apartment. Owning a co-op requires very little maintenance but provides little privacy, and typically you will pay more expensive HOA dues.

We examined the difference between custom, semi-custom, and production homes. The important point to remember is that the cost of the home does not ensure quality construction. The same subcontractors building $80,000 homes will be working on $1,000,000 custom homes. You also learned that production homes and semi-custom homes come with a large variety of upgrades available today.

We explained homeowner's associations (HOAs) and covenants, conditions, and restrictions (CC&Rs). It is extremely important that you know what these documents say before you buy. You must know all of the rules of a community to be sure it fits your lifestyle before you move in.

Finally, we discussed the difference between resale value and salability. Determining the features that you have in your home can have an effect on the resale value of your home. The three most important rules to remember are location, location, and location. Never buy a home in a suspect neighborhood, no matter how good the deal seems to be.

Chapter 2

Can You Pay for What You Want?

In this chapter:

- How to Find a Good Lender
- Brokers versus Direct Lenders
- Fees, Points, and Closing Costs
- Types of Loans: Fixed Rate, Adjustable Rate, Nonqualifying, VA, and FHA
- Determining Eligibility Using Ratios and FICO Scores
- Benefits of Preapproval
- Timeline: Application to Closing
- Questions for the Loan Officer
- Chapter Summary

Now that you have at least an idea of the type of house you want, the next step is deciding how to pay for it. We've all seen the ads on television and the Internet, explaining just how simple it is to get a home loan. They make it sound so easy—all you have to do is call them, and in ten minutes you have a home loan, right? Wrong!! Competition between these lenders is just plain vicious. That's why, to say the least, their ads tend to exaggerate the truth.

The truth is that your credit and income are extremely important, no matter what they say in their ads. Your total household earnings and all your bills are figured into ratios, which determine how high your monthly payment can be for your home. In addition, lenders use a system called FICO (**F**air **I**ssac **CO**mpany) scores. They look at your FICO score along with your ratios and credit report, and then they add in other circumstances you may have to determine your complete eligibility for a home loan. It can sound very confusing at first, but let's walk this road together. It's much more enjoyable to hunt for your new home when you know exactly how much you can afford to spend versus getting out there, falling in love with a house, and then discovering you can't afford it. We want you to enjoy every step of this journey. When you finish this chapter, you'll have the Insider's scoop on understanding the loan process, finding a good lender, getting the best loan, and closing on your home.

How to Find a Good Lender

All loans are not the same, and that can be said about lenders, too. When you are shopping for a lender, you will see several ads that offer the "best personal service," the "lowest rates," and the "quickest loan approval time." These are like campaign promises: They are easy to make, but also very easy to break. Through the years, we have worked with many lending institutions, including direct-lending companies and mortgage brokers. We've also worked with literally hundreds of loan officers, loan processors, and different types of assistants too numerous to mention. One thing is clear: It can be very hard to find the ones who really do give the service that they claim. Here are some Insider guidelines to help you with your decisions.

First Guideline: You want to know how many new loan programs a lender offers; a good lender will have several. It is also important to know whether you are dealing with a broker or a direct lender who funds the loan. If you use a broker, you should be aware that a completely different company will be making all of the final decisions. We cover the differences between these two in the next section of this chapter.

Second Guideline: It's important to get a list of all the fees the lender charges. This list is called a "Good Faith Estimate." We go into detail about fees and estimates later in this chapter, too.

Third Guideline: You will want to interview the lender's representative, the loan officer. You will find a list of interview questions at the end of this chapter. This list will guide you through the loan officer selection process. Some of the information you will be discovering is how much experience the loan officer has and how many builders he or she has worked with in the past. A loan officer who has worked with new homes might even know of a certain builder's quality or lack of quality and whether they complete their homes on time. One national builder that we know of tried to force homeowners to close on their homes before the drywall was installed (i.e., the wood framing was showing). The builder wanted to increase his quarterly profits at the expense of about 30 homeowners. Fortunately, the experienced and reputable loan officer who handled the majority of these homes refused to close unless the homes were completely finished. In this case, it was the loan officer and her company who saved several homeowners from a lot of sorrow and grief.

Fourth Guideline: You want the loan officer to be accessible for questions. Many loan officers will be more than willing to talk to you when taking your application, but once they have secured your loan, it can be very difficult to reach them by phone. It can be very frustrating to need an answer to an important question and not be able to reach the loan officer. Instead, you may reach an assistant who cannot answer your question, so you will still need to call the loan officer to get your question answered. This is not to say that speaking with an assistant is always bad. We've worked with many who were very knowledgeable and helpful. Sometimes, though, you want to talk to the "head honcho," and you need to make sure you can. If during your research you find out that most of your contact will be with the loan officer's assistant, you will want to meet him or her too before making your final decision.

Insider Tidbit:

Almost all loan officers are paid on a commission basis; they do not get paid until your home closes. Contrary to how it may seem at times, loan officers really do their best to get your loan approved. They don't get paid for disapproved loan applications, so the more loans they close, the more money they make. This commission structure is good for you because it creates competition between the lenders. Competition between lenders gives you the opportunity to shop for the best deal in town. But what is the best deal? Is it the lowest rates? What about points and "junk fees"? Remember— the best deal is not a deal at all if your loan officer cannot perform and deliver on her promises.

Fifth and Final Guideline: Find a loan officer who can be trusted and who gives 110% effort and dedication until the loan process is finished and your house has closed. We want to share with you one simple example that should give you a good understanding of what we mean. The last loan officer we used before retiring from the new-home business was Claudine Branchaud. Claudine works for a mortgage company in Las Vegas, Nevada. Remember, we said there are two kinds of lending professionals in the real estate industry: the ones who claim great service and the ones who actually provide it. Claudine is the latter. By the way, Claudine knows that we will be telling this story.

> It was about 4 P.M. on a Friday. We had a new-home buyer in our office, and we wanted some general information about a lending program. We knew Claudine always kept her cell phone with her, and we were accustomed to calling her at any time, on any day of the week. Claudine answered this particular call with a very sickly sounding, "Hello, this is Claudine, may I help you?" We said, "Claudine you sound terrible. Are you sick?" She slowly replied, "Yes, I am sick. It looks to me like I have strep throat. Right now, I am in the doctor's office, getting a shot of penicillin." You can imagine our reaction to her answering the phone in her current situation. If you have ever had strep throat and had to get a shot of penicillin, then you can visualize the image of the position Claudine was in when answering our call.

Our point in telling this story is not to embarrass Claudine but to show you how dedicated she is to her profession. Having a dedicated, competent loan officer can mean all the difference in the world when in comes to getting your home closed properly with no glitches. Take another look at the picture on the opening page of the "Introduction." This home was financed with an FHA (Federal Housing Authority) loan and should never have closed without the proper FHA appraisal. However, the lender managed to pull strings and got it closed. Any good lender would never have let this happen. The homeowner thought she had a great deal with the mortgage broker she used to finance her home. Her "great deal" turned out to be one of the factors that allowed her house to be delivered to her in such a terrible condition.

Overall, we've been talking about good lenders who provide good service. To find these good lenders who provide the service you need, start by asking friends and relatives for referrals. A good Realtor can also be a source of lending referrals if the Realtor specializes in new homes. We would feel good about a Realtor who has read this book or attended one of our instructional workshops. You may look in the newspapers and yellow pages if you can't get referrals, but remember the "Rule of Three." Whether you get referrals or not, always interview at least three lenders before deciding which one will finance your home.

When making your final decision on a lender, compare the information from your research of the lender and their loan officer with the costs of the loan program that you want. For example, you may want a 30-year fixed-rate loan. Lender "A" offers a lower interest rate of 7.5%, charges 2 points, and your contact person is the loan officer's assistant. Lender "B" offers the higher interest rate of 8%, charges 1 point, and has a great loan officer as your contact, plus they have more experience financing new homes. You must compare the costs of the loan with the amount of service that you will be getting. Once you have chosen the best lender and loan officer and picked the best loan program for you, you're ready to apply for the loan.

Insider Tidbit:

If your loan officer does not live up to her promises, you can always change loan officers, or lenders for that matter, even up to the day before you close on your home.

Brokers versus Direct Lenders

When shopping for lenders, you will come across several mortgage brokers. Mortgage brokers are companies that process your loan application and then look for a direct-lending company to finance the loan you want. The name of the company does not always identify it as a brokerage. It may simply be called "XYZ Mortgage Company." You have to ask the loan officer if she is a broker or if her company actually funds the loan. With only one exception, we do not recommend using a broker to get your loan. There are several reasons why we recommend using a direct lender instead of a broker.

A broker is a middleman: They process your loan application but do not fund or loan any money. They take your paperwork to other companies looking for one to fund your loan. This is referred to as *brokering out* the loan. The company that funds your loan is the lender. Remember, we said a loan officer with the lender gets paid commission on each loan that she closes. A broker also gets paid commission on a loan; that's how they make their money. The broker makes her commission; the loan officer makes her commission; and the lender makes a profit off the loan, as well. This will always result in higher costs for the loan. Guess who gets to pay those higher costs? The borrower—you. You may pay more in points, junk fees, or an origination fee, but somewhere in those fees everyone is making their commission and profit.

When using a broker, you may never know who is making the final decision on your loan. Most brokers use several different lenders to get loans/mortgages approved. Sometimes, the broker is not always familiar with each lender's requirements. More than once we have had a home closing delayed because a broker did not meet the lender's requirements. Who loses in this situation? The homeowner. You will always lose because it is your closing and your home that can be held up. Imagine having to send your moving truck back with all of your furniture to the moving company and paying several hundred dollars a day in storage fees until you can get your loan closed. On top of that, ask yourself where will you live in the meantime. Do you think your mortgage broker is going to pay for your storage fees and hotel bills? Not likely. We have seen too many new-home buyers stuck in this position far too often.

An Insider knows that the broker has no approving authority. If you ask your broker a question about your loan, the broker may have to go back to the lender to have it answered. This sounds simple, but remember the broker is a middleman. Think about this: You finally make contact with the broker and ask your question. Your broker in turn has to call the lender and speak to the loan officer there. Then the loan officer has to get back to the broker, who in turn has to get back to you with the response. This can take a lot of time, sometimes days. When you are getting ready to close on your home, time is of the essence. You need to be completely sure that everything is ready.

Another difficult situation we have seen is when a brokered loan is approved at a certain interest rate. Then that rate is drastically raised right before the closing of the home because one of the lender's conditions wasn't met—usually because the broker was either not aware of it or they weren't paying attention.

Earlier we stated that we do not recommend loan brokers, with one exception. Here is that exception. If your credit is very poor and you cannot find a direct lender to give you a loan, then you might still be able to get your loan through a broker. We have seen brokers find loans for people whom most lenders would not even talk to. These loans will have high interest rates and fees, but it may be your only option if your credit is very poor. Some of the large lenders will even broker out a loan rather than turn you away, if it is really difficult to get approved under their guidelines. If you are credit and cash poor and really want that house of your dreams, then a high-interest loan might be worth it to you. After two years of establishing good credit, it might be possible for you to refinance your home with another lender at a much better rate.

We have come down a little hard on mortgage brokers, but we are only speaking from experience. We do, however, want to remind you that it is possible to find a good, honest, hard-working mortgage broker. There are brokers that can perform very well, but our experience has taught us to approach loan brokers with extreme caution. If you fall into the high-risk loan category, then a broker might be able to help you more than some of the larger lenders who traditionally have higher requirements for approval. You just need to understand that a brokered loan will always cost you more. If you do end up using a loan broker, be sure to *get absolutely everything in writing,* and you must get references. Remember the "Rule of Three."

Fees, Points, and Closing Costs

Fees

Insiders know there are two types of fees that lenders may charge for their services. First, there are *legitimate fees* or charges for such services as appraisals and full credit reports. The lender has to pay for these appraisals and credit reports, and the cost is passed on to you. However, there are other fees that are not legitimate, and these are called *junk fees.* Junk fees are extra charges just to increase the lenders's profit on the loan. Common names for junk fees are *processing underwriting, document preparation,* and the like. When you are interviewing potential lenders, ask if they charge any junk fees. The loan officer will immediately say no, whether she had intended to charge the fees or not. She now realizes that you are knowledgeable about the lending process, and she has just gained instant respect for you. You never want to pay junk fees, and they can always be negotiated out of the deal.

Several lenders will charge an *origination fee* to obtain the loan. This fee is usually 1% of the loan value. For example: You get a mortgage for $100,000. One percent of the loan value is $1,000, or 1% of $100,000. The origination fee allows the lender to make a profit on the loan, and it is considered a legitimate charge. However, if you end up paying an origination fee plus points, you are going to have very expensive closing costs. Insiders would never pay an origination fee plus points to get a loan. The only exception to paying both would be to obtain a very low interest rate.

There is one fee that is optional with most lenders and can provide a great savings for you. It is called an *interest rate lock fee.* Most lenders will lock your interest rate for 30 to 60 days for no charge. This means if your house closes during this period of time, you have a guaranteed interest rate. Remember, interest rates can go up or down each day depending on several factors in our economy. Many a new homeowner has bought a new home when interest rates were great only to have them go up drastically before the house was completed. The unhappy homeowner thought he was getting a 7.5% loan because that's what it was when he signed the contract for the house and when he got his loan approved. Unfortunately, he finds out the rate has gone up to 8.25% when his house is done and it is time to close on his loan. This situation can be avoided completely by locking in the interest rate. If your house is going to take six months to complete and current rates are great, you may want to pay a fee to lock in the current rate for your home. Your loan officer should be helpful to you in deciding when it's best to lock in the rate. Charges for this service will vary from lender to lender, but it is one of the questions that you will be asking prospective lenders when conducting interviews.

Points

Points are another very important charge to consider. They are charged as a fee to get a certain loan. They can also be charged to buy an interest rate down to a lower percentage. Points will be charged the exact same way that the origination fee is charged. It will be based on your loan amount. We have seen some great interest rates in the Sunday real estate sections of newspapers across the country. However, if you look in the points or the origination column of the paper, you can see a charge as high as 3.5 points. Lenders can make a loan sound great by offering interest rates much lower than the current going rate. These interest rates are called *teaser rates,* because they are teasing you with what seems like a great offer. The lender is hoping that you will ignore the fees and points and just concentrate on the low interest rate. Insiders always compare all fees and points with interest rates. A loan with a low interest rate may seem like a good deal if you just consider the interest rate. However, once you add the fees and points, you may end up paying more for the loan than if you had gotten a loan with a higher interest rate but paid no points or origination fee.

Let's do a comparison. Take a look at the two loans in Table 2.1. In loan B, you would have to pay $1,000 at closing—the cost of one point for the lower interest rate. It would take you 29 months to make up that cost in your monthly payment savings. This would probably be a wise investment. Let's say that the same loan charged you two points instead of one. Now it would take you 58 months to make up your initial cost. If you took the $2,000 that you would pay in points and put it into a mutual fund, you might get a much better return on your money.

You might be wondering right now what would happen if you paid three or four points. Could you buy down the interest rate from 8% to about 6%? No, it doesn't work that way. The

Table 2.1   Cost of Point Analysis

Loan A		Loan B	
Amount of loan	$100,000	Amount of loan	$100,000
Interest rate, no points	8.0%	Interest rate, 1 point	7.5%
Monthly payment	$733.76	Monthly payment	$699.21
Cost of points	$0	Cost of points	$1,000
		Monthly savings	$34.55
		Months to recoup cost of points	29

lower the interest rate goes, the more it costs to buy it down. In the example in Table 2.1, we paid one point to buy down the interest rate .5%. It went from 8.0% to 7.5%. If you paid another point, you would most likely reduce the interest rate by only an additional .25%. Reducing the interest rate gets much more expensive as you go lower. In most situations, if you are going to be in your home for at least five years, it would be a good financial move to pay one point to buy down the interest rate .5%. We would not recommend paying any more in points unless you would get at least a .5% reduction in your interest rate. Your loan officer can give you several scenarios and explain the advantages of each to you.

Closing Costs

Closing costs are all of the costs you must pay when closing on your home. These costs will include all of the previously mentioned fees and all other costs, including your down payment on the house. When you apply for a loan on a house, you will receive what is called a *good-faith estimate* from your lender. Your loan officer will give you a form that lists all charges you must pay. This will include junk fees if there are any. The lender estimates your down payment and all other payments necessary for closing, such as taxes, escrow fees, and insurance. This estimate will give you a good idea of just how much money you will need to close on your home. If your loan includes points or origination fees, your closing costs will be much higher. When you receive this list, ask your lending officer to explain every cost to you. This way, you can identify junk fees and negotiate to have them eliminated. Once you can see all of the closing costs in front of you, it will help you decide if you want to pay any points to buy down the interest rate or pay an interest rate locking fee.

Insider Tidbit:

Everything is negotiable. You may only want three incentives on a deal, so ask for six. That way even if you don't get the six incentives, you should at least get the three that you really wanted.

Types of Loans:
Fixed Rate, Adjustable Rate, Nonqualifying, VA, and FHA

When you apply for a loan, you need to realize there are several different kinds of loans available. You will need to choose not only the one that you qualify for, but also the one that gives you the best deal. Lenders have become very creative with the boom in the new-home industry over the last several years. We cannot address every type of lending program that is available today because there are just too many. Knowing what type of loan would be the best for your situation is another function that your competent loan officer will be able to help you determine. A good loan officer can explain the benefits that are attached to each program. Everyone has different circumstances that will affect the type of loan they will want to get. A program that is great for one buyer might not be very good for another.

Once you have chosen a qualified and competent lender, you will need to make an appointment to fill out an application. Remember our last loan officer, Claudine? We have seen her take a loan application in our office with her notebook computer, hook up to our phone line, and have a complete approval letter generated on the spot. The whole process had taken less than two hours. If you can get this type of service, you are doing very well. Normally, the application process takes longer. You may not actually get a loan approval for 72 hours or even longer if you use a broker.

This whole process will be less stressful if you can get a list of required information and documents from the lender *before* you show up for your appointment. Many lenders will have a complete application packet for you to fill out that also lists the required documents that you will need to bring to the appointment. The closer you follow the lender's instructions, the less time the application should take. In addition to processing the forms you complete, the lender in most cases will make a credit check and verify your employment. These two items will add to your wait time for a loan approval, especially if the responding parties don't reply quickly. We have seen reputable lenders give complete loan approval within 72 hours. It will be very difficult to get this type of service from a broker. Remember, the broker is the middleman and not the approving authority.

In the following sections, we will be discussing the most widely used loan programs: the fixed-rate loan, the adjustable rate, nonqualifiying loan, the VA loan, and the FHA loan.

Fixed Rate

The fixed rate is the most common loan program. Most home buyers get a 30-year loan at a fixed interest rate. This means that the interest rate stays the same for all 30 years until the house is completely paid off. For example, you buy your house for $125,000. You pay $10,000 for a down payment on the house, and you need to finance the remaining $115,000. Your loan will be $115,000 at a fixed rate of, let's say, 8% for 30 years. With this program, your monthly payment of principle and interest (P&I) would be approximately $844.00. Your payment would never change for the next 30 years as far as principle and interest go. This loan program is comforting if you get a good rate because you know your payment is never going to go up. It is also a good program for people who plan to stay in their home for a long time, such as 15 years or more.

You can also get a fixed rate for a 15-year mortgage, and usually you will get a .5% reduction in the interest rate charged. This will lower the amount of interest you pay the lender, but it will increase your monthly payment because you will be paying off your house in only 15 years. Let's compare these two loans by reviewing Table 2.2.

As you can see in Table 2.2, the 15-year mortgage would increase your monthly payment by $222, but look at the total amount you will have paid at the end of the life of each loan. If you took the 15-year mortgage, you would save $111,960, and you would completely own your home in 15 years. If you could afford the extra $222 a month for your payment, it might be your best

Table 2.2   30-Year versus 15-Year Fixed-Rate Loan

30-Year Fixed Rate at 8%		15-Year Fixed Rate at 7.5%	
Amount financed	$115,000	Amount financed	$115,000
Monthly payment (P&I)	$844	Monthly payment (P&I)	$1066
Total amount paid after 30 years	$303,840	Total amount paid after 15 years	$191,880

option. We are not saying that you should select this option, but we just want you to see how different the results can be when selecting your loan program.

Adjustable Rate

The *adjustable rate mortgage* (ARM) means that it will adjust over the life of the loan according to the terms you agree to follow. It might be a better loan option for you depending upon your circumstances. There are several different types of adjustable rate mortgages. Terms like 7/1 ARM or 3/1 ARM refer to the number of years the interest rate is set and when it will start adjusting. Let's look at a 7/1 ARM; here's how it works. The first number, 7, refers to the first seven years the buyer would have a fixed low interest rate, usually about 1% lower than a 30-year fixed rate. The second number refers to how often the interest rate will adjust, after the first seven years. In this case, every year (1-year increments) the interest rate will change. The adjustment can go up, down, or even stay the same depending upon the criteria set by the lender for that ARM. Usually, there is no prepayment fee for this program; this would allow the homeowner to refinance the home at any time.

In Table 2.2, we compared two loans that assumed you would be in your new home for at least 15 years. Table 2.3 takes the same house and compares the 30-year fixed rate to a 7/1 ARM, assuming you were only planning on staying in your home for six years.

As you can see, not only would your monthly payment be $79 lower, but also after six years when you sell your house, you will have saved $5,688 on the total cost of your home. This is just an-

Table 2.3   30-Year versus 7/1 ARM

30-Year Fixed at 8%		7/1 ARM at 7%	
Amount financed	$115,000	Amount financed	$115,000
Monthly payment (P&I)	$844	Monthly payment (P&I)	$765
		Monthly savings	$79
Total amount paid after 6 years	$60,768	Total amount paid after 6 years	$55,080

other example of how important it is to select the right program for your situation. This example also stresses the importance of having a good loan officer who understands several programs and is willing to take the time to get you the best loan program that suits your needs. There have been too many times that we have seen loan officers more interested in getting the loan closed and not necessarily in getting the buyer the best loan available. Insiders always research the different programs and do not work with a loan officer who cannot explain each option clearly.

Nonqualifying

There is another type of loan that has been very popular in recent years. This program is called the *nonqualifying loan*. It is also called a *no document* loan because there is very little paperwork to be completed in the application. The applicant does not have to meet income standards and ratios that conventional loan applicants would have to meet. This loan can be used for people who make a good living and have a lot of cash but cannot verify their income under conventional standards. For example, an applicant may be self-employed and unable to show a two year history of qualifying income because they recently opened a new business. As an applicant, you still need an excellent credit rating; this will be determined by your FICO (**F**air **I**ssac **CO**mpany) score. We will discuss the FICO score in detail in the next section. It requires a detailed explanation because virtually every lender uses this score to determine loan eligibility on almost every loan program.

To obtain a nonqualifying loan, the applicant must have a good FICO score, and it also helps to have good compensating factors. These factors may be residence stability, as in living at your current address for more than two years, and verifiable money in savings or investments. You may not have a job, but you may have a large bank account from an inheritance, or you may own stock that you don't want to sell at this point. If your FICO score is good, the lender will usually want a 10% down payment from you to get the best interest rate available. We have seen down payments as low as 5% for nonqualifying loans, but the interest rate rises sharply with a lower down payment. This loan also works well for people who have just moved into a new area and cannot meet the two year work history requirement for a conventional loan (i.e., fixed rate, ARM, VA, and FHA).

VA

The VA (Veterans Administration) loan is available to anyone who is considered by the administration to be a veteran. This means the applicant has served in the military and was given veteran status upon being discharged, or the applicant retired from military service.

This loan program provides the incentive of a very low or no down payment to purchase a house, along with a fixed interest rate comparable to a traditional loan. It is good for the lender, too, because the VA guarantees 25% of the loan amount up to $205,000, which means little risk to the lender.

The new home will also undergo special inspections dictated by the administration in an attempt to ensure a quality built house. These inspections cover very specific standards, from how the house is constructed to what level of appliances are included. Not all builders will accept a buyer with a VA loan because they don't want to deal with these additional inspections, or they know they cannot pass them.

There are a few downsides to a VA loan. One is a limitation on the total loan amount allowed for the guarantee. At the time of this writing, the maximum loan amount allowed by the VA is $205,000. This means that the VA will guarantee 25% of $205,000. If the loan amount is higher, then there is no guarantee on the amount above $205,000. Also, there could be a limitation on the kind of upgrades you may finance into the loan based upon their value. Talking with your loan officer should help to clarify how these situations may affect you. If you do get a VA loan, remember that if you choose the dollar-down option, it will be very hard to have any equity in your home if you had to sell it within a few years after buying it. You should review this financial scenario with your loan officer if you know you will be in your home less than five years. You may still decide to go with the VA loan but have a higher down payment, or you may decide a different loan program makes better financial sense for your situation. If you are not sure if you would be eligible for a VA loan, ask your loan officer for details, or call your local VA office.

FHA

The FHA loan (Federal Housing Authority loan) is very well-known and traditionally associated with a first-time home buyer.

The appraised value of the house will dictate whether an applicant can use this loan program. At the time of this writing, there is a $130,000 cap on what the total amount of a loan can be under the FHA program. This program offers benefits to both the lender and the borrower, just like the VA loan does. For the borrower, an incentive is extra protection in the form of inspections and a lower down payment, usually only about 3% of the cost of the home. The FHA also has required inspections on the house, and they require an FHA appraisal before the loan can close. This is supposed to protect the home buyer and the lender, but Insiders know these inspections and appraisals don't always happen as they should. Take another look at the house in the "Introduction." This house was financed with an FHA loan, and the appraiser must have done what we call a drive-by inspection. In other words, the appraiser just drove by the house to see if it existed. In this case, we also know that the second-rate lender and loan officer involved did not wait for the final FHA inspection approval. Beware of less than reputable lenders; they will take advantage of programs like the FHA and VA, which were meant to protect you.

Insider Tidbit:

The borrower, you, will be paying for PMI (private mortgage insurance). The lender will require the borrower to carry this insurance whenever there is less than 20% paid for a down payment on a loan. This insurance protects the lender and not you. If you default on your loan and the lender has to foreclose on the house, then private mortgage insurance helps pay the cost of the home until the lender can resell it. There is one exception: VA loans carry their own guarantee. There is no PMI charge on a VA loan. FHA loans do not have PMI, but they have MIP (mortgage insurance premium). It is exactly the same thing under a different name. Be aware, once you have paid 20% of the value of your loan to the lender, you can have them remove this insurance. However, you have to ask! The lenders will never offer it to you unless you ask.

Determining Eligibility Using Ratios and FICO Scores

After the loan application is made, the lender should be able to tell you how much you can afford as a monthly payment. Two major factors are used to determine your eligibility for a home loan: ratios and FICO scores.

Ratios

There are two specific ratios that we will discuss: front end and back end. These ratios are the comparison of your total household monthly income to your monthly bills. This comparison produces a percentage figure; these percentages are the ratios. When we speak of these ratio figures, we are talking about what the lenders consider as guidelines.

To figure a front-end ratio, divide the total monthly payment for the new house, or PITI (**P**rinciple loan payment, **I**nterest on the loan, estimated property **T**axes, and estimated house **I**nsurance), by your total monthly income. The number you come up with will be a percentage number. In our example in Table 2.4, the PITI of $1,000 is divided by your income of $4,500, and your front-end ratio equals 22%. This is a good ratio because generally lenders prefer to see a number of 28% or less.

Now let's figure the back-end ratio. Here we add your monthly household bills to the PITI to get your total monthly bills at the new home. Please be aware that lenders will only be using the monthly bills that are considered long-term commitments and debts that will take you six months or longer to pay off. This means that your credit card minimum payment amount will be

Table 2.4   Front-End and Back-End Ratios

Total monthly income	$4,500	
New-home loan (PITI)	$1,000	Front-end ratio: $1,000 ÷ $4,500 = 22%
Car payment	$225	
Credit card	$45	
Personal loan	$35	
Total monthly bills at new home	$1,305	Back-end ratio: $1,305 ÷ $4,500 = 29%

counted as a bill unless you can pay it off within six months. It also means that something like a cable bill will not be included in your monthly bills because it is not a long-term requirement.

To continue figuring the back-end ratio, we'll take this new monthly total (your bills plus the PITI) and divide it by your total monthly income. In the example in Table 2.4, the total of monthly bills at the new home, $1,305, is divided by your income of $4,500. The result is your back-end ratio of 29%. We're doing great because lenders prefer to see this ratio at 36% or less. Generally, 36% is a safe ratio to use when trying to consider how much home you can easily qualify to buy.

Notice we said that lenders would *prefer* for you to stay within their ratio guidelines. We have seen ratios go as high as 36% on the front end and as high as 50% on the back end. What would make the lender be more generous on the ratios? Remember that there are several compensating factors that can help the applicant, but the biggest influence of all is the FICO score.

FICO Scores

The most influential factor that practically every lender uses today is called the FICO score. FICO is an acronym that stands for the **F**air **I**ssac **CO**mpany. This company invented a system and developed a computer program that is used to determine just what kind of a risk an applicant might be at a particular point in time. The Fair Issac Company will not divulge how their formula works because they consider it proprietary information. They would not want another company stealing their formula.

When you apply for a mortgage, your lender will send in a credit application to one or all three credit reporting agencies. These agencies are Experian (formerly TRW), Equifax, and Trans Union. When your credit report is returned to your lender, it automatically includes your FICO scores. Even though all of the credit agencies use the same computer program, your scores could be different because each score is based on data that each credit agency has on you. You will not be able to get an exact explanation of just how the FICO score is determined from any lender. In fact, most loan officers don't even know exactly how the score is determined, but they do use it. Some loan programs are not available unless your FICO scores are high enough.

FICO scores can range from 300 to 900, but getting a FICO of 900 is virtually impossible. There are very few applicants that score above 800, and usually the average score will run between 550 and 750 points. The FICO scores are meant to be a prediction of whether you will pay your loan back on time. A higher score means you are a better risk than someone with a lower score. For example, if your FICO is 680 or higher, you would probably be considered a good risk and qualify for the best interest rates available. However, if your score was below 620, you might not qualify for a loan at all; if you do, you will likely have a higher interest rate charged.

Although we cannot tell you exactly how they compute your individual score—no one can—we can give you an idea of how your FICO score is achieved. At the time of this writing, the biggest issue in calculating your FICO score is your credit history. If you have had good credit in the past, it will make your score higher. Poor credit will obviously make your score lower. FICO scores look at three parts of your credit history: severity, recency, and frequency.

Severity of your credit refers to the type of delinquency you may have on your credit record. Obviously, if you have a 90-day late payment on a credit card bill, it is much more severe than a 30-day late payment. A 90-day late payment will bring down your score much more than a 30-day; just how much is not known. It may be possible to have a higher FICO score with two 30-day late payments than only one 90-day late payment. The bottom line is the later your payments are, the more severe the deduction on your score. If you have a bankruptcy or repossession in your history, it will greatly affect your score. Again, just how much is unknown.

Recency refers to when the delinquency occurred on your credit. If you had a late payment three or four years ago, it will be much better for your score than if it occurred within the last year. Also, your FICO score will be higher based upon how long you have had credit. Let's say that you have had two credit cards for seven years. If you have a good payment history with these two cards, then your FICO score should be higher than a person with the exact same cards and payment history, but they have only had them for two years.

Frequency in your credit history means how often the delinquencies occurred. If you had one late payment on one credit card, it will be a lot less significant than three or four late payments. The lender wants to know how often or frequently you have made late payments. Frequency also refers to how often you have credit inquiries from companies. Your FICO score will be affected each time you apply for credit and when these applications occurred. Did you apply for every credit card offer in the mail in the last two years? If you did, you will have a credit inquiry for each one on your credit report. It does not matter if you received the credit card or not. Too many inquiries will hurt your score.

Here's an Insider story: Several years ago, we bought two new cars from a dealer before we were in real estate and understood how FICO scores worked. The dealer assured us he would get a great financing rate with one of his several lenders; he did just that. Little did we know that he sent the credit applications to nine different lenders his company used. All nine of these credit inquiries showed up on our credit report. A year later, we applied for a home mortgage and found out our FICO scores were dramatically reduced because of these inquiries. Remember, every time you apply for any credit, like when applying for a cell phone calling plan or car insurance or even a small clothing store credit card, you will be adding another inquiry to your credit record and possibly lowering your FICO score.

Insider Tidbit:

Did you know that if you have too many credit cards it can actually hurt your FICO score? The reasoning is that you could go out, charge several thousand dollars after closing on your home, and then not be able to afford the loan payment. The increase in your credit card bill makes your ratios much higher, and you become a much higher credit risk. From our experience of seeing hundreds of credit reports, it seems that the best number of credit cards to have is from two to five; this number includes the small store cards along with the big names like VISA and MasterCard. If you have over seven, it will start to hurt your score even if they are paid on time. If you have fewer than two, it will help you to have additional credit sources to support your credit history.

Ten years ago, if you wanted to buy a house it was pretty cut and dried as to the process. There were no FICO scores to use, and there weren't half as many loan programs as there are today. You would basically apply for a loan, and you would expect to put 20% down on the house. If your credit was good and you earned enough to make the payment, you would probably get the loan. Today it is a much different world. Not only are all of the factors mentioned previously taken into consideration, but lenders now consider compensating factors also. Lenders today will consider alternative sources of credit that they would not have considered ten years ago. Examples would be utility bills. You can get letters of credit history from your utility companies showing years of timely payments. These letters can establish a good credit history even if you have never bought anything on credit. However, note that lenders usually require a two year history for these bill records.

Remember that the FICO score is a tool the lenders use to help them decide whether or not to lend you money. We have seen loan programs from lenders that would not budge an inch when the FICO-required score was not met. In other cases, we have seen lenders disregard the FICO if the applicant had other compensating factors. The reason we have spent so much time explaining the FICO score is because right now in the industry, it is the most important factor in getting approval for your home loan. We have ended this section with some "Do's" and "Don'ts" that should help to positively effect your FICO score.

Do's

- *Pay off all bills and loans on time.*
- *Check your credit report to ensure that it is accurate.*
- *Keep your credit card limits low.*
- *Follow your loan officer's advice on how to improve your score. (It can change monthly.)*

Don'ts

- *Don't have more than five credit cards.*
- *Don't max out all of your available credit.*
- *Don't apply for any new credit for two years before applying for a mortgage.*

Loan qualifications, just like loan programs, can vary greatly from lender to lender. The guidelines we have discussed are only to let you know where you might stand. In no way should you use these to make your final decision as to whether or not you should apply for a loan. You must talk to a good loan officer for specific information to make that decision. Remember, credit is only one of the factors used to determine your overall eligibility, and your ratios can vary due to compensating factors in your life. We have seen good loan officers work miracles for clients who never thought they would get their loan approved.

Benefits of Preapproval

You will hear the term *preapproval* when you start researching lenders. You will also hear the term *prequalified*. The two terms, although sounding similar, are completely different. Prequalified simply means, based on what you have verbally told a lender, that they have determined you should qualify for a loan for a certain amount. The lender has not verified anything about you at this point; typically, they have only computed your ratios. If you approach a new-home agent and tell her you are prequalified for a loan, she won't give it much consideration. Insiders know that anyone can be prequalified just by talking to a lender, and it means nothing. Prospective buyers can, and do, tell lenders many tall tales, to put it nicely. It is not until the lender verifies everything and does a thorough credit check that the complete truth comes out.

Several times we have seen loan applicants suddenly remember their bankruptcy after the credit check revealed it. In one case, we actually had a married couple apply for a loan to buy a house in our community. The wife had clean credit, but the husband said he had a couple of late payments that might show up. When the credit check came in, it verified he did have late payments—one of which was several years of not paying child support from a previous marriage. His current wife had no idea he had been married before, let alone that he was a deadbeat dad. Once all this information came out, the couple was turned down for their loan by their lender. The wife was so mad at her husband's dishonesty about everything that she divorced him, came back, and bought the house on her own. When this couple first came into our office, they had been prequalified by their lender. Suffice it to say that there is no benefit in being prequalified.

On the other hand, preapproval is a completely different situation. When you are preapproved by a lender, it means your credit has been checked and all verifications have been made, as well. Complete loan approval means the lender has made a commitment to lend you money. Once you are preapproved for a loan, you can get a letter from the lender that will state the amount that you are approved to borrow. This letter can be a good negotiating tool to use when buying a new home; this is one benefit for getting preapproved. One of the biggest concerns for the new-home agent is your ability to get a loan. If you can show a preapproval letter, the agent knows she has a qualified buyer. She will work extra hard to keep you. We cover the negotiation for your home in chapter 8, but a preapproval is one factor that can help you get a better deal.

Please understand, when we mention preapproval, we are talking about getting it from a well-established and known lender. Preapprovals from a broker may not be very helpful unless the new-home agent has worked successfully with that broker in the past. A preapproval from an unknown lender or broker will be considered suspect and may not be worth the paper it's written on. In our experience, there have been too many times when unknown lenders and brokers could not deliver the loan promised to the buyer in their preapproval letter, and the whole deal fell apart. If a client came in to our office with a preapproval letter from an unknown lender or broker, we would give it little if any weight at all, and most of our colleagues would do the same.

On top of all this, every builder will have a preferred lender they will want you to use. Some larger builders even have their own mortgage companies. The builder wants you to use their preferred lender because of the influence they have with that lender. The builder and new-home agent want to know immediately if you are loan approved, and the builder's lender will report directly to the builder and agent to let them know. As new-home agents, when we sold a home and the buyer used our lender, we knew there would be no last minute glitches at closing. We know when our buyer was approved that it was a legitimate approval and it wouldn't fall apart at the last minute. If the buyers used their own lenders, we would lose that direct information link and control. When we called the lender for information on the home loan, we sometimes would get the run-around or end up dealing with less than professional people. The last thing that we wanted to happen was to have a deal fall through at the end because of an incompetent lender, but it happens. That is why new-home agents want you to use their lender to maintain better control of the situation. (As you will learn—throughout this book, new-home agents always want to be in control). The builder wants you to use his lender for the same reasons, plus the fact that the builder will get a little better deal on closing costs from his preferred lender. Because the builder is sending all of his business to one lender, then the lender in return gives the builder a discount on the seller's closing costs.

You many wonder at this point if preapproval is worth getting if the builder and new-home agent are going to push for their own lender. It is true that the agent will want you to use her lender, but she wants to sell the house even more. If she knows you are preapproved from a well-known competent lender, she won't mind if you use your own. You may be aware that you have the right to pick your own lender, and the builder cannot force you to use his. This is true; the builders cannot force you to do anything. On the flip side, if the builder doesn't like your lender, he will simply make it more advantageous for you to use his lender rather than using your own.

This is how it works. Let's say you are looking at a house, and the builder is offering 1% toward closing costs as an incentive to buy it. The home you are looking at costs $150,000. One % of the home price would be $1,500. This sounds great, doesn't it? Now here's the catch. You only get the 1% ($1,500) if you use and close escrow with the builder's lender. The builder is in no way forcing you to use his lender, but you will be giving up $1,500 if you don't. Some builders are very strict about giving any incentives at all unless you use their lender. This is where your pre-approval letter from a competent lender comes in. If you present the letter and say you want to buy the house and still get the incentive, most builders will agree if they can trust your lender. The builder's main goal is to sell the house. If your preapproval letter is from Agent #2003 of LoansRus.com or from Aunt Jane who works part time at Joe's Mortgage Company, it will be very difficult to make the deal. It will depend upon the builder's experience with these companies. Preapprovals can definitely help you as long as they come from trusted and respected lenders in your area of the country.

One other benefit of a preapproval letter is to put your mind at ease. The anxiety of wondering how you'll pay for the new home you are searching for can drive you crazy. It can be very disappointing to find your dream home only to learn you can't afford it. We highly recommend finding a good competent lender (remember the "Rule of Three"). Once you find that lender, get preapproved for the maximum amount that you can. Insiders realize they don't have to spend the whole amount. Think about it, if you are preapproved for a loan of $150,000 and you find a home costing $130,000, your preapproval letter looks that much stronger to the new-home agent. This can help you even more when negotiating the deal.

Let's say you have set a limit of $130,000 that you want to spend for the base price of the house. Now you have decided that you want to add some additional structural options into your home loan. Wouldn't it be nice to know if you would be able to do this before starting out on your search? The answer is a resounding yes! The more you know before heading out, the less stressful it will be. This book is all about relieving stress by preparing you to make the best deal on your new home. Getting a preapproval letter from a competent lender is just one of the steps toward that goal.

Timeline: Application to Closing

The first step is to research lenders and loan officers to find the best one to fit your needs. After you have selected one, you will make an application for a loan. This application should be made before you start looking seriously for your new home. You should understand that your preapproval would only be good for six months. If you have not closed on your home during this time, your lender will need to update your loan status. Lenders will need to get updates of their information every six months. These updates are called *reverifications,* and they are necessary to make sure your loan qualification status has not changed.

Once you have a preapproval letter, you will know how much house you can afford. You want to stay preapproved. Remember the ratios that determine your payment? What happens if you go out and buy that new car you have been wanting? If your new car payment is higher than your previous payment, it can change your ratios. We have seen qualified buyers purchase houses and then buy a new car or other expensive toys that immediately disqualified them for their home loan. In other cases, this did not completely disqualify them, but they were overextended on their credit so it did raise their interest rate. Remember the FICO scores? If you raise the amount of debt that you have, you also raise the amount of risk you are as a borrower. A lower FICO score could also mean a higher interest rate for your loan, and who wants higher interest rates? We can't think of anyone, either.

Staying qualified after getting your preapproval letter is very simple. If you plan on buying a new car, a boat, or even several Christmas gifts on your credit card, just talk to your loan officer first. She can tell you how much you can spend and still remain qualified. She could also advise you not to spend a dime and wait until after your home has closed. After your escrow closes, it doesn't matter what your ratios are. Don't try to buy something and hope your lender doesn't find out about it either. Many lenders run another credit check right before closing to make sure nothing has changed in your status. If a new car loan shows up on your credit report, it might disqualify you for your loan and cancel the closing on your new home. It could also end up hurting you by raising your interest rate. If you try to cancel the sale because of higher rates, you will lose your earnest money and any money that you gave the builder for options. All of this can be avoided by keeping a good honest relationship with your loan officer. If you have followed the guidelines in this chapter about selecting a lender and keeping qualified, then the closing process will be painless, at least where your loan is concerned.

Next, you find your dream home after following all of the steps in this book and sign the purchase agreement with the new-home agent. You give her a deposit check, typically written out to the title company that the builder has chosen to use. The title company's escrow officer will open your escrow account when they deposit your check. Now the builder gets to work on your house.

As far as the lending and finance steps are concerned, the next relevant action will be after the home is completed. You attend the walk-through orientation of your new home that is usually scheduled by the new-home agent. We will be discussing the walk-through in detail in chapter 10, but because you are reading this book, we know your walk-through will be perfect.

The next step is attending your title appointment. Your new-home agent will have set up this appointment, too. She will relay the date and time for you to go to the title company. All of your paperwork will be there for you to sign; nothing will be missing because you have selected a good, competent lender. Either your loan officer or the title officer will contact you at least two days in advance of this appointment to let you know the exact amount your cashier's check will need to be. This check will cover your loan down payment and closing costs. Once you sign all of the documents and give the cashier's check to the title officer, your part of the loan process is complete. Normally this appointment lasts about 60 to 90 minutes.

Insider Tidbit:

Never go to your title appointment before attending your walk-through.

After you finish at the title office, your lender will "fund" the loan; this is when they give the money to the title company. The lending part of buying a new home is now over. The title company takes the money and pays the correct parties and now your escrow closes. They will also record the title, actually going to the county recording office and submitting the paperwork that changes the ownership of the property from the builder to you. It will either record that day or the very next day. After the recording takes place, the house will actually be yours. Only after it is recorded will you get your house keys.

Questions for the Loan Officer

When you start your search for a lender and loan officer, we suggest you ask these questions. We recommend calling the lender and asking for a loan officer experienced with new-home builders. Once you are connected with this loan officer, you can ask these questions over the phone, or by appointment. Remember, you are going to talk to at least three loan officers.

- What hours can I reach you by phone?
- Will you always return my calls if I get your voicemail?
- Will I be working with you directly or an assistant?

- How many new-home loan programs do you have?
- Does your company fund the loans, or do you broker them out?
- Who makes the approval decision on my application?
- How long will it take to get loan approval?
- How long can we "lock in" an interest rate at no cost?
- Do you charge any junk fees?
- How many new homes have you financed?
- What local builders have you worked with?
- When will I receive a good-faith estimate?

Chapter Summary

We have covered a lot of information about the lending process in this chapter, but it is meant to give you an overall understanding of the process. Knowing the importance of having a good loan officer and a reputable lender cannot be stressed enough.

Today there are dozens of loan programs available, and we touched on just a few. Your good loan officer will be able to offer you the best program available for your needs. Insiders depend on their loan officers not only to get the best loan, but more importantly, to provide the best service.

You should be able to figure out approximately where you stand on qualifying for a loan using the formula for ratios we presented, but remember that the ratios for loans can vary depending on the lender and compensating factors. Also, you should know that your FICO scores are the single most important factor that will affect your eligibility for a loan. A good loan officer can help you improve these scores in addition to following the "Do's" and "Don'ts" in this chapter.

Finally, we went over a timeline of the loan process from start to finish. You first need to conduct interviews using the loan officer interview questions and the "Rule of Three." The next step is to make a loan application; after getting approval, you need to stay qualified. Once the home is complete, a good loan officer will make sure your loan is ready so you can close without any glitches. Insiders hate glitches, and we are going to make sure that you don't have any.

Chapter 3

Where Do You Want to Live?

In this chapter:

- What Is a Good Location?
- School Zoning
- Traffic
- Master-Planned Communities
- Flood Zones and the Environment
- Is There an Association?
- Which Lots in the Community Are the Best?
- Neighborhood Questions
- Chapter Summary

By now you should have a good idea of the type of house you want and approximately how much you can spend on it. So what are you waiting for? Most people would be out of the door looking at model homes by now. We know you're eager; in fact, you probably have already been looking. That is just fine as long as you haven't made any commitments to buy. We need to talk about a few things that relate to where you want to live.

What Is a Good Location?

You've heard the phrase be fore, "location, location, and location." It still applies today. But, just what is the best location? What makes it the best? The first half of the answers to these questions will be decided by your personal desires. The second half of the answers concerns appreciation in property value and several neighborhood benefits that may be overlooked. We are going to bring up a lot of questions about location to help you think of everything that is important to you and also everything that might increase the value of a neighborhood.

If you are moving somewhere new, then you might consider hiring a Realtor to help you with your search. We will talk at length about using Realtors in chapter 4. Right now, we want to show you how an Insider chooses the best location for their new home. Insiders understand that some locations in cities appear to be nice areas, but when examined closely they really are not the best places to live.

As an Insider, start off by listing (yes, another list) what you need to be near and what you want to have around you. Is it important to be close to parks and schools? Do you need to be near a freeway or train station? There are hundreds of little things that can be important to you. For example, you may have a simple list like:

"Needs and Wants" Neighborhood Wish List

I need to be within a 30-minute drive to work.

I need a park I can jog in every morning.

I need to be close to the airport.

I want to have a grocery or convenience store only 15 minutes away.
I want to be within 20 minutes of a major mall.

I want to live in a gated community.

Do you remember your needs and wants list in the first chapter? Of course you do, because you probably have already filled out this list and changed it three times. You are using the same principle here, but this list will be about your neighborhood instead of features in your home. You may list 30 needs and 40 wants—the more you have the better. The closer you can match your list in a community, the happier you will be moving there. This gives you some parameters to gauge the communities you will be considering. If you think you might have found a neighborhood that comes close to matching your list, then you can take the next step.

Start from the community that you are interested in and drive in every direction for two miles. You are looking for obvious and subtle things of what is around you. You must go at least two miles. If you drive only half of a mile away, you might miss the graffiti on the next street or the abandoned factory only a mile away.

As you drive in each direction, you are not just looking for evidence of gang activity, but you are going to look for the items on your list—things you'll eventually need, like mailboxes, post offices, gas stations, or maybe a library where your children can do their homework. (*Your children will love you for this thoughtfulness.*) When you find the grocery store, stop in and look around. Is this a store where you would want to shop? Is there a convenience store close to your community? Will you have to drive more than 15 minutes just to get a gallon of milk? Is that acceptable? Are there other new-home communities in your area? Does the neighborhood look like it is new and growing, or does it look like it's depressed and run down? Following your needs and wants list and using common sense, you'll get a good picture of the whole area.

If you have any doubts about the area around the prospective community, ask yourself if you would be comfortable driving through this neighborhood at night. You should also visit the neighborhood at night to see what it's like. Does it have enough light, or too much light? Do you feel safe? Also, would you feel comfortable about your spouse or children traveling through this neighborhood? Be aware that the specific community you are looking at might be wonderful, but if you have to drive through a bad neighborhood to get to it, that bad neighborhood might spread into yours. You must drive the two miles in each direction, making sure it is comfortable for you. Insiders know that many neighborhoods can look wonderful from most directions except from the one less traveled. That's the one direction that might be a haven for bad elements.

School Zoning

If you have children, then you definitely want to know how close the schools are. Schools vary in their rules for determining how close you can live and still let the kids ride the bus. We have seen communities that were beautiful and were only 1¾ miles from great schools. This appeared terrific to the families, too, until they discovered that the school would not provide bus service to anyone who lived within two miles. What seemed like a convenience quickly turned into a problem for the families with limited transportation or where both parents worked. Now they had to find time to drive the children to school and pick them up, or let them walk.

School zones can and do change in a growing city. If it's important for your children to be in a particular school, then you must check with the school zoning board to see if any changes are planned for the future. We have seen many people buy their new homes in certain neighborhoods mainly because of the school, only to have the school zoning change before they had even moved in.

What if you don't have children? What if your list of needs and wants says you don't want to be next to a school? What about school speed zones near your home? Think about them, too. Imagine your day if your school lets out when you're coming home from work or worse, when you are trying to get to work. Schools and the speed zones near them can create some pretty major traffic jams.

Traffic

When most people go out looking at new homes, they do it on the weekend, on a Saturday or Sunday. This is of course when most people are not working and school is out. Insiders realize that the traffic they experience on a Saturday is not going to be the same during the week. If you are looking at a beautiful community and the location seems perfect, consider what it would be like during rush hour. How will you get to the stores and restaurants? What will your "work route" be? The biggest issue for most adults is getting to and from work. If you are really serious about the community, then you must take a test drive of the work route during rush hour. Pick one morning and one evening, and actually drive to and from the neighborhood. You will be much happier finding out about any big traffic bottlenecks before you buy the home rather than after you move in. Traffic could be the deciding factor if you can't make up your mind on two different communities.

As you figure out the best traffic routes, you need to consider what it will be like in the future. If you are buying in a neighborhood that is building up rapidly, then you have to wonder what will happen to the traffic after those other communities are sold out. Are there plans to widen and/or add roads to improve traffic when everything is finished? How long might that take— weeks, months, or years? Also, where are the on and off ramps to the freeways? Is there one close by now? If not, will there be one in the future? Will it be too close? You don't want to buy in a neighborhood that will have a freeway built so close that you constantly hear the traffic. At the same time, you may not want to be so far away that you have a driving nightmare getting to and from work. For most people, driving to work takes a considerable amount of time out of their daily life. Most people, us included, want this time to be as quick as possible. If you have to drive through a traffic bottleneck every morning from your perfect new home, we guarantee that new-home perfection will soon tarnish.

Master-Planned Communities

Master-planned Communities or *master plans,* for short, have become very popular in several cities across the country. A master plan is basically a plan for the whole neighborhood that contains the new-home community. It can include schools, stores, hospitals, and parks as a part of the plan. Master plans can offer several amenities, such as pools, golf courses, and community centers; however, with every amenity it offers, there will be an increase in the homeowner's association (HOA) dues. If a master plan is done right, it can be a dream neighborhood to live in, as long as you want the special features that are included. We have seen master plans that include nothing except some common landscaped areas. There are also master plans that include everything you will find in a small city. If you are looking for a Master-planned Community, you need to find the one that offers the amenities that you want without paying for several things that you won't use.

Remember, the more amenities that you have will result in higher HOA dues. Do you really think you will use a community pool, or will you want one in your own backyard instead? If you don't have children, will you receive any benefit from having a youth center? Your neighborhood wish list that you created in the previous section of this chapter will help you decide if a master plan will be what you want. But, don't get taken in by everything that is included in a master plan unless it is everything that you really want.

In large master plans, there are usually several builders who will build separate neighborhoods within the master plan. For example, in Las Vegas there is a gigantic master plan called "Summerlin." This master plan has been under construction for over five years and will probably continue for another ten years. This community is made up of several new-home builders and also contains hospitals, shopping centers, office buildings, several parks, trails, and even a resort hotel casino. In a large development such as this, many individual neighborhoods will have their own HOA, and you will be required to pay dues. This HOA will be subject to Summerlin's HOA, and you will also have to pay dues to the Summerlin HOA, as well. Summerlin can be considered a dream neighborhood to live in, but it is only a dream if you don't mind paying two HOA dues, being subject to the two different HOAs, and their rules agree with your lifestyle.

We need to mention a term called *local improvement district (LID)* or *special improvement district (SID)*. These terms, commonly referred to as LIDS and SIDS, are special assessments levied by the city to pay for the infrastructure necessary to develop a new-home community. By imposing a LID on a new-home community, the new-home builder will have to pay for the infrastructure instead of the city. This cost is passed on to the new-home buyers in the form of a monthly assessment that usually lasts for about 15 years. We have seen LIDS and SIDS vary in the amount charged, and it is according to the location of the property and the size of the lot that the home buyer purchases. Several master plans have these assessments, and you will need to ask the builder's agent if there are any when you are looking at homes.

In different parts of the country, LIDS and SIDS may have several different names. Although the names may be different, they are assessments just the same. Not all master plans have special assessments, but they will be more common in large new-home community areas. We just want you to understand what the assessment is for, should you encounter one.

Flood Zones and the Environment

In your new-home search, you may see communities built in a flood zone. Why would anyone build a new-home community in a flood zone, you may ask? Because the land is less expensive, and there is a bigger margin for a builder's profit. If you look at models in a flood zone, the new-home agent may tell you something like it is only a "100-year flood zone." She will make it sound like there is only a flood every 100 years. We have worked for FEMA (Federal Emergency Management Agency) as disaster assistance employees, and we have been sent to numerous "100-year flood zones." It may be true that on the average the area will only flood once every 100 years, but this area can also flood three times in one year if the conditions are right. There is no guarantee that if you live in a flood zone that your house will not flood several times, and it only takes once to destroy everything that you own. Flood insurance can rebuild the structure of your house, but it can never replace your personal items. As experienced disaster workers and new-home experts, we have one simple but very important statement concerning flood zones. *NEVER, UNDER ANY CIRCUMSTANCES, BUY A HOME IN A FLOOD ZONE.* Did we make our point? You just can't depend on the weather enough to risk your home.

You may not live in a flood zone, but are there any drainage ditches or washes close to where your home will be? Hopefully you spotted them, if any, on your two mile orientation drive. If you're not sure, ask the new-home agent about it. Let's say there is one. What happens if the wash becomes cluttered with debris, and a heavy rain comes? That wash could overflow, and your home could end up with six inches of water on the floor. There is a good reason early settlers built on high ground. You should use the same caution when selecting your neighborhood and home site. Don't be fooled by transformational vocabulary that the agent might use to try to cover up a wash; it is used to describe a negative feature in a more positive light. We will talk more about this technique in chapter 5. A good agent can turn something negative like a flood zone completely into a positive feature simply by how she describes it. We have also seen this technique used to fool experienced real estate professionals. True Insiders will not be fooled, and you are going to be a true Insider.

There are other environmental factors to consider in addition to flood zones. When you drove the two miles around the community, did you see any factories or production plants? What do these companies produce? Are there any emissions put into the air that may be unhealthy, or are there any smells or sounds you don't want to have to endure? These companies may be closed on weekends when you are visiting a new-home community, but during the week you might awaken to machinery that they may start at 6 o'clock in the morning. Is this the kind of alarm clock that you want?

Is There an Association?

We have talked about associations (HOAs) before, but you should always remember to ask about it when you are considering a new-home community. Associations can vary to a great degree in what they cover, and the new-home agent will rarely understand everything in the HOA's rules. Insiders, under most circumstances, want an association in the community where they live. The HOA can enforce rules that will keep your neighborhood nice, and without them there is no guarantee that your neighbors will take care of their homes. You may take immaculate care of your house, but if your neighbor doesn't, it not only becomes an eyesore but it can also bring down the value of your house. A few irresponsible neighbors could affect your whole neighborhood. We all want to live free of rules, but it is the opinion of the authors that associations in moderation are a necessary evil. You want protection for your investment, but you don't need extremes like the "Garage Police." Take the time and learn the HOA rules and CC&Rs before you buy. Make sure these are rules you can live by.

Which Lots in the Community Are the Best?

In a new-home community, there will usually be several different-sized pieces of land called *lots* that are available for you to choose from. The builder has what they call a standard-sized lot and premium lots. Premium lots have extra costs added on to the base price of a home in consideration for getting a larger space, or a more desirable location such as being on a corner, or for a view.

Be careful if you are paying more for a lot just to have a view. There have been many homeowners that have paid high lot premiums for views only to have them blocked by future construction around their home. You must know what is being built in front of your view to make sure you'll always have what you are paying for. If you pay a lot premium for a view, make sure that your contract states that fact. If you pay for the view, it should always be there.

Construction is not the only way that you may lose a view. In one community in Las Vegas, homeowners paid $60,000 per lot for views of the Strip. When they moved in, the view was fantastic of the whole city. What they didn't count on was the older community that lived slightly below them on the hill. This community had maturing trees that eventually grew up and blocked their beautiful views. This situation certainly urges good relationships with the neighbors, especially regarding their landscaping. But, if you want a view, you must look at every aspect of the surrounding area.

Corner lots are usually a little larger than the standard-sized lot and are more desirable because you only have a neighbor on one side. Corners are good for resale because there is a bigger demand for them than for a house that has neighbors on both sides of it. Lots on cul-de-sac streets are also more desirable, especially for families with children. If you live on a cul-de-sac, there is no through traffic; this makes it a much safer area for children because of the minimal traffic. When you are thinking about the resale of your home, remember that the more demand there is for the home and its location within the community, the higher the resale price you can ask for it. Cul-de-sacs appeal to families, and families are the greatest number of buyers of single-family homes.

When you pick out your lot, find out which model home will be behind you and on both sides of you. Whether you choose a single or a two-story home, ask yourself if the house behind you is a two-story how much privacy will you have in your backyard. If you will be down the hill from your backyard neighbor, how much privacy can you create? Keep in mind, depending on the size of your yard, your neighbors behind you could be looking right into your bedroom.

The direction that your house faces can be important as well. Remember, most designs for houses have the majority of windows in the back and front of the house. If you are buying in an area of the country where there is a lot of heat from the sun, you may want your house to face north or south. This will allow the sun to pass directly over your house instead of shining directly into the front or back windows. With less sun shining into your windows, it will be easier to cool the house and keep the utility bills lower. If you live in a cooler northern climate, you may want the house to face west or east to get more sunshine in the winter and avoid the northern wind blowing into your windows to help lower heating costs.

When choosing the lot for your home, you know that some lots will have premiums added to the cost of the home. You may have asked yourself, are these premiums negotiable? Absolutely! Premiums are known as an extra profit for the builder. He doesn't have to pay a subcontractor for a lot, and he doesn't have to buy any materials for it either. The builder just assigns a premium to a lot because he thinks he will be able to get it. We've seen builders claim they are charging the premium to cover the cost of "developing the land," like putting in retaining walls or slopes. This is a case of attempting to collect twice for a cost. Builders should have already included these "development costs" into the initial cost analysis of the community and included them in the base price of the houses.

We have also seen premiums of $30,000 dropped to $5,000 during negotiations. In many cases, an Insider will be able to get the lot premium eliminated altogether. When you make an offer on a house, always try to get the lot premium eliminated from the deal. You may not always succeed in getting it completely eliminated, but you should almost always be able to get it substantially reduced. For example, you are looking at a standard-sized lot that is next to a green grass area on one side, so you don't have a neighbor on that side. The builder thinks this lot is worth $10,000 due to the "extra privacy" the homeowner will have. An Insider would offer to buy the house with no lot premium because the lot is not any bigger than a standard lot, and the builder didn't pay any more for that lot than any of the rest. The agent on site will try to negotiate a better deal for the builder, but she may accept your offer without paying any premium at all. If you end up negotiating, an Insider would never pay more than $5,000 for this particular lot. If the builder would not cut at least 50% off the lot premium, the Insider would not buy the home; it makes us question the builder's money situation. This situation would be different if the lot was larger than the rest. A larger lot can justify a premium, but even then the premium can be negotiated down. Remember, lot premiums are only based on what the builder *wants* and not on any of the builder's costs. You as an Insider have *wants* too, and you want to save money on lot premiums.

Neighborhood Questions

The following questions are here to help you develop your "Needs and Wants Neighborhood Wish List." You will think up several wants and needs on your own, and these are just to help you add to your list.

1. *What is in the two mile surrounding area?*

   Is there any graffiti? Where are the stores? Where is the nearest fire station? Where is the closest emergency care or hospital? Is the area growing or does it look run-down? Will you be comfortable having your children pass through this area?

2. *Are there any environmental factors?*

   Are there any industrial buildings within two miles? What do they produce? Will there be any unpleasant noises or smells? Are you near any drainage ditches? Could they back up and flood your house?

3. *What about traffic?*

   Will your drive to work be difficult? How long will it take to get to your favorite restaurant? Are there freeways or expressways near by? What about bus stops, train stops, and train tracks: Any nearby?

4. *What is the school zone?*

   Is your teenage son or daughter just going to die because they have to change schools? Do you like the schools that your children will be attending? Is there bus service, or are you going to have to make time to drive your children to school? Do the speed zones change near your home?

5. *How does it feel?*

   Do you feel at home in this neighborhood? Is this a place that you will want to come back to? Would you feel good having your friends come into this neighborhood to visit you? What does it look like at night? How is the lighting? Is there a park nearby? If yes, what condition are the grounds in? Who pays to keep up the park?

6. *Associations*

    Are there HOA dues? What are the rules and CC&Rs? Does the HOA enforce these rules or a management company? Does it look like the rules are actually enforced?

Chapter Summary

When you are looking for a neighborhood, the main consideration is where you *want* to live, and that decision is up to you. In this chapter, we have tried to mention some factors that a lot of people do not think about until it's too late. Environmental factors such as a noisy production plant or a drainage area that could result in flooding of your home might be missed without careful observation. Of course you would *never* buy a home in a flood zone, no matter how good the deal seems.

Checking the traffic during the week will also give you an accurate picture of your future commute to work. You will want to make sure that your school of choice is zoned for where you are moving, and it is not due to be changed.

Obviously, you want a nice area. You would never buy in an area that even looks marginal. Remember, areas seldom improve, but they can go down very quickly. You don't want your new-home community to look run-down just a few years after you move in. Your HOA will help keep this from happening, but you must pick the right area to start with. When you get serious about a community, you will always read the HOA rules and the CC&Rs.

Finally, the issue of "location, location, location." It is a culmination of all the issues we've discussed in this chapter. It revolves around choosing qualities and amenities that many people would agree are positive and remain that way while you live there. Ultimately, the best location will be determined by your personal wants and desires.

Chapter 4

Realtors, Do You Need One?

In this chapter:

- How to Find a Good Realtor
- What Is a Buyer's Agent?
- Can You Fire Your Agent?
- Can a Realtor Save You Money?
- How Does the Builder See Realtors?
- Do You Have the Time to Do It Yourself?
- Realtor Interview Checklist
- Chapter Summary

Before you can decide if you want or need a Realtor, it's important to know just who Realtors are and what they can do. You may have heard the terms *agent, Realtor,* or *broker.* A real estate agent is someone who has passed the state and national real estate exams and has been granted a real estate license. A real estate agent may work directly for a builder as an employee to sell new homes as a new-home agent. Or she may decide to go into business for herself and become a Realtor who works with buyers and sellers of property. A Realtor may not open their own business under their own name. The Realtor must work under a broker's license, so the Realtor becomes an independent contractor who works for a broker. Brokers are the bosses of resale. They are real estate agents who have also obtained their broker's licenses. This license, along with other state requirements, allows brokers to open their own real estate offices.

Almost all real estate agents who sell resale (preowned) homes are Realtors. The term *Realtor* is a designation given to members of the National Association of Realtors (NAR). This is a nationwide trade organization that promotes education among its members as well as other services, such as the multiple listing service (MLS). The MLS is vital to the selling and buying of resale homes because it lists all homes for sale that are represented or listed by other Realtors. The MLS is of very little use when it comes to buying a new home.

What is important to understand is that Realtors are not new-home agents. Realtors are trained in selling, or "listing," resale homes and helping clients (buyers) find a home. Listing a home means that a Realtor has signed a contract with a homeowner to sell their home, and they will "list" it in the MLS. New-home agents are trained to sell new homes for a builder and are not usually members of NAR, so they do not have the designation of Realtor.

What about the Realtor who advertises herself as a new-home specialist? The following requirements are necessary to make this claim: buying business cards and printing "New-Home Specialist" on them. That's it. Realtors may claim they are new-home specialists, residential specialists, or any kind of specialist that they like. But there are Realtors who really can help you in your new-home search. Let's show you how to separate the real specialists from the pretenders.

How to Find a Good Realtor

If you are a home buyer, you want to pay close attention to the following information. If you are a Realtor, then you are about to learn what we would expect your service to be. This book was created to give our home buyers the advantage of Insider information. It is giving the reader the best information and service that is possible today. We will expect nothing less from you if you are a Realtor. We want to teach you what you can do for your clients. We want to share with you Insider information and a complete guide to providing the best service out there. We know there are a lot of Realtors who honestly want to give the best service possible, but just don't quite know how to do it. If you are truly willing to work hard for your clients, then the following guidelines are for you. If you are not willing to work hard, you might want to pass this book on to another Realtor who is fully committed. We realize that many Realtors would rather get listings than work with new-home buyers. There is no shame in feeling this way. We, on the other hand are only interested in Realtors who are dedicated to their buyers and who want to specialize in new homes. If this sounds like you, then read on.

The first step in finding a good Realtor is to ask her if she has read this book. We realize that you are truly progressive, and you may be one step ahead of your prospective Realtor. She can order our book direct from the publisher or purchase it from the bookstore of her choice. Remember, this book is the only one that reveals Insider information, and you definitely want your Realtor to be as smart as you. We don't recommend that you give her your copy of the book because you will want to refer back to it several times in your new-home search. Make her buy her own copy or have her check it out of the library. Once she has read this book, she will know what you expect of her and just how hard she is going to have to work. A good Realtor will not balk at hard work.

If you become a happy homeowner and she is part of the reason you feel this way, then the Realtor will feel happy and proud of a job well done, not to mention earning herself a well-deserved commission along the way. Happy homeowners refer their friends and relatives to Realtors who have performed well, and that's how they build their business. The next step to finding that great Realtor is knowing what she must do to earn your satisfaction and your referral. All of these services will be explained in detail as they are discussed in different chapters of this book. As we cover different subjects, we will make a reference that Realtors can perform this service. These references are only to highlight to the Realtor what their specific expected duties are, but these "duties" are yours if you do not have a Realtor.

- Preview builders in areas where you might want to live. Your Realtor should visit prospective new-home communities before you do. If you need a five-bedroom house with a three-car garage in four months, then your Realtor should not be taking you anywhere that these houses do not exist.
- Do preliminary builder research. Get reports from the Better Business Bureau and state contractor's board.

- Drive you to all new-home communities that may fit your wants and needs. You should never make the first trip to any new-home community without your agent.
- Negotiate on your behalf. With the information in this book, your Realtor will know what incentives she will be able to get.
- Support the Homebuyer's Protection Addendum. Your Realtor should try to get the builder to include this addendum in the contract you sign.
- Research the builder and superintendent. Knock on doors of other communities. Find out where the superintendent has previously built and check those neighborhoods for quality.
- Be present when choosing your options, to negotiate on prices.
- Videotape the construction of your house. The Realtor can spend a lot of time watching and filming the construction. Superintendents will always do a better job when they know some one is paying attention.
- Meet with the superintendent. You and your Realtor should be on a first-name basis with your superintendent.
- Be present at the frame-walk. You and your Realtor will be present for the walking inspection of your new house at the framing stage.
- Be present for your final walk-through. You want your Realtor to be there when you do your final walk-through because two sets of eyes are better than one.
- Finally, your Realtor should be with you at your closing appointment just in case anything unusual comes up.

You want your Realtor to be willing and able to perform all of these services. You may share in the videotaping, the builder research, or any of the other guidelines, and that's fine. However, if you don't have the time, then you must be able to depend on your Realtor to perform without the slightest objection.

The last step is the interviewing process. Just like you did when looking for lenders, ask for referrals and, if necessary, look in the phone book or advertisements. When you are interviewing Realtors, remember the "Rule of Three." Even if you fall in love with the first person you meet, please, always interview at least three. Use the Realtor interview checklist at the end of this chapter. Everything you want to know about your Realtor is in that checklist.

One of the questions in your interview list will be about experience. We want to make the point here that being inexperienced is not always bad. In fact, we have known many new Realtors who were eager to do everything for their clients. If a Realtor looks good to you on everything except experience, don't pass her up. This book will give her all of the new-home experience that she needs. A new Realtor will have more time to devote to you because she will not have too many other clients. If you are her first client—it means she will give all of her attention to you. Combine this book with that much attention and she will be a real asset for you. We would much rather have a new Realtor giving 100% effort than an experienced one who can give only 50% effort.

What Is a Buyer's Agent?

You may see Realtors advertise themselves as a buyer's agent. A buyer's agent only works for clients looking to buy a house. They don't handle selling/listing of houses. This is an important distinction in resale, because you wouldn't want the same agent representing you as the buyer and also representing the seller of the house. Neither of you could have a fair representation. When buying a new home, you will be dealing with a new-home agent who works for and represents the builder. This agent has a fiduciary responsibility to get the builder the best deal possible. If you hire a buyer's agent, then she will have the same responsibility to you. If you do decide to use a Realtor, then you would want a buyer's agent. If you pick an agent who has several listings in the MLS, they will take up a lot of her time; this could be time away from you. If you want to go house-hunting, you want your agent to be available.

A good buyer's agent may want you to sign a *buyer's broker agreement*. This agreement means you will be responsible for paying the agent a commission on your home at closing. Actually, you don't usually pay this commission because there will be a clause in the agreement that allows the builder, or seller, to pay it. But, it is very important for you to realize that you are responsible for paying this commission if the builder refuses to do so. It is rare for the builder to refuse to pay the Realtor, but we have seen it happen. This might occur if you went to a new-home community the first time alone, without your Realtor. Builders pay Realtors for being the procuring cause of the sale. Simply put, you wouldn't have bought the house if it weren't for the Realtor; it's like paying a finder's fee. The Realtor found you, or in your case you chose her, and she brought you to the builder. If you go to a new-home community on your own, then your Realtor wasn't the procuring cause for the sale. The builder is justified in refusing to pay your Realtor's commission, and if you have a buyer's broker agreement, you will be responsible to pay it. It is very easy to avoid this scenario; you must always be taken to new-home communities by your Realtor on the first visit. Your Realtor will then register you at the community, and you can go back as many times as you like after that by yourself.

Insider Tidbit:

New-home agents typically have great memories. If you try to sneak in to see the models and then return with your Realtor later, the builder could stand firm with the verbal statement from his agent that you were alone on your first visit and not pay the commission to your Realtor.

We feel that if you find a Realtor who meets all of the standards in this chapter, then she deserves to be protected with a buyer's broker agreement. Besides, if she were doing her job, then you would never be visiting a community for the first time without her. You are going to demand a lot of hard work from the Realtor you choose. It is up to you whether or not to sign a buyer's broker agreement, but if your Realtor is going to commit to you, isn't it only fair that you commit to her, as well?

Can You Fire Your Agent?

Let's suppose you take every step in this book and hire a Realtor. After a couple of weeks or months, something happens—like her enthusiasm disappears, or she won't return your calls, and you haven't seen much of her lately. Can you fire your agent? Yes, at any time.

Insiders would never sign any agreement that would not allow you to terminate her services with notice. We suggest a 30-day written notice in the agreement. Sometimes what seems to be a good working relationship just goes south. It could be a personality clash or maybe some personal hardship in her life. Whatever the reason, we would suggest that you call her and talk to her. If she isn't in her office and she won't return your calls, then talk to her broker.

Remember, the broker is the boss. Tell the broker about the treatment you are getting from your agent and that you wish to terminate your buyer's broker agreement immediately. The broker will handle the cancellation, as long as you had it written in your agreement. She will also remind you that if you buy any of the houses that your Realtor took you to, then you will still be liable to pay her commission. Some buyer's broker agreements ask for this protection for up to six months. We suggest that you try to negotiate this period of liability to only 90 days when you sign the buyer's broker agreement. This protection is necessary for the Realtor because there are unscrupulous people who will hire Realtors to take them around town, and after they find the house they want, they try to fire the Realtor and cut them out of the deal. We have seen this happen on several occasions. Insiders would never do this, and we don't feel you will have any problems because you are going to be asking for a lot of information during your interview. With the screening process that you will use, you should eliminate any possible problems before they arise. If you don't have anything in writing like a contract with your Realtor, then it is just a matter of a phone call to cancel your relationship.

Be aware that builders will still pay a commission to the Realtor you just fired because she was the procuring cause of your being there; this is a separate issue from your buyer's broker agreement period of liability. The builder's time frame for how long they will plan to pay the commission varies between them. Typically, it's about 30 days from the time the Realtor registered you into their community or 30 days from the last visit she attended the community with you. If you decide to get another Realtor and bring her to the same community, you need to understand what the builder's time frame is. If you bring the second Realtor in too soon, she may be out of luck for a commission. Typically, the builder will only pay the first Realtor when you sign a contract for purchase within that initial registration period. Always try to remember that the builder pays the Realtor who was responsible for bringing you into the community.

Can a Realtor Save You Money?

If you have a Realtor who is doing everything stated in this book, then the answer is yes. There are a lot of uneducated Realtors who don't do much more for their clients than provide taxi service. Insiders would never use such a Realtor. But a Realtor who is going to research the city and find a deal that you may not have otherwise known about is going to save you money. Realtors can relieve stress by handling most of the details of your search. On top of that, a Realtor who takes the time to go out to your house every week and film the construction process is going to save you money because you are going to get a quality built home. A quality built home will cost you much less in future repairs.

Some people are not comfortable with confrontation. In order to negotiate a good deal, you must be able to be firm and a little confrontational at times. If you don't feel you are able to do this, then a strong Realtor will save you money. The biggest question that you will ask yourself after finishing this book is whether or not you have the time to perform all of the techniques in this book. You definitely want a quality built home, and a Realtor can help you achieve this, but would you be able to save even more money if you didn't use a Realtor?

How Does the Builder See Realtors?

Most builders want Realtors to come to their communities. We have worked for builders who have gone out of their way to attract Realtors. Builders know when a good Realtor brings in her client, because that client is "ready, willing, and able to buy" (Insider phrase). Notice we said good Realtors. We are not talking about the taxi-service Realtors. We have had great relationships with good Realtors who have brought back several terrific buyers. Builders don't mind paying a commission to Realtors who bring in good business, and they want them to keep coming back.

Sometimes we have had people come in trying to negotiate a deal to get the commission that the builder would have paid if they had a Realtor. The buyers felt that they should get the commission because the builder had it budgeted to be paid on every house. This is unfortunately a false assumption. Insiders know that builders do not plan to pay Realtor commissions on every house.

When a builder opens a community, he will usually plan on selling up to 40% of the homes with Realtor participation. The other 60% of the homes he expects to sell without Realtors. This means that on 40% of the homes, he plans to pay a commission of usually 3% of the base price of the home. This commission is sometimes considered just a cost of doing business. It's planned for in the following manner. Let's say there is a community of 100 homes that sell for $200,000 each. The builder plans on paying a commission on 40% (40) of the homes at rate of 3% for each of the 40 homes. The total commission cost for this community would be figured like this: 3% of $200,000 = $6,000. $6,000 × 40 = $240,000. Now the total commission cost for this community is $240,000. If you divide $240,000 by the total number of homes, which is 100, you get $2,400. In this community, the builder has budgeted about $2,400 to spend on a commission charge for each house. As long as he doesn't go above 40% on commission payments, he will stay on budget. Builders rarely want more than a 40% cooperation rate with Realtors, and they do not plan to pay a commission for each house. So, if you don't use a Realtor, you will not get a commission because the builder doesn't have it for every house.

Now, having said that, what about the $2,400 that the builder averages into each home? If you are looking for a home without a Realtor and want to negotiate a deal, you may be able to get a slight reduction in the house simply because you do not have a Realtor. It won't be the 3% commission amount, but it could still be worth a couple of thousand dollars.

How can you get part of this amount? First, you need to understand how the negotiation process works. When we received offers from buyers, we would then present these offers to the builder's representative, who is usually the vice-president of sales. The first question she would ask is, "Do the buyers have a Realtor?" She wants to know if there will be a commission involved in this sale. If there is, she will not give away as much money or incentives as she might without a Realtor. This additional amount that she will work with, when there is no Realtor, will vary between builders, but a good rule of thumb would be about 1% of the purchase price. In our experience, we have seen thousands of deals offered, and a good offer might be able to get 1% more if a Realtor is not involved in the deal. This means on a $200,000 home that you might be able to save $2,000 on the purchase price if you don't have a Realtor as part of the deal. If you aren't using a Realtor, you must remember that you will be the only one negotiating as well. Could a Realtor have come up with another way for you to save money? This would depend on your negotiating skills. You also have to take into consideration the fact that you may not have even found the house you are negotiating for if it hadn't been for your Realtor. The bottom line is a good negotiator will probably get a better price for the home without a Realtor even though builders will never confirm this fact. You just have to ask yourself if a Realtor is willing to perform all of the services stated in this book, and is she worth that 1%?

Do You Have the Time to Do It Yourself?

As you read this book, we are going to tell you everything that you can do to get a quality built home at the best price possible. When we say the "can do" part, we are talking about taking actions, and some of these actions will take time. It takes a lot of time to locate the perfect house for you to buy. It will take time to knock on doors to research the builder and the superintendent. It takes time to visit your community to film the construction process of your home. If you and your spouse both work long days and long hours, you may not have the time to follow the guidelines stated in this book. You may not want to take the time to follow our advice. If you don't follow all of our steps, it doesn't mean that you cannot get a good deal on a home. It simply means that for every step you leave out, you lessen the chances of getting the best price or, more importantly, you might lessen the building quality of your new home. Every step we teach you is proven to be of great benefit to you. If you don't have the time to follow the steps in this book, then a Realtor might be worth far more than the 1% you might have lost when negotiating the deal.

Realtor Interview Checklist

- Have you read *The Ultimate New-Home Buying Guide,* and are you willing to follow all of the steps in the book? (This is the most important question, because this book will outline all of the Realtor's expected duties.)
- How can I reach you? Phone? Cell phone? Beeper? E-mail? Do you always return your calls if I have to leave a mes-

sage? (The number-one complaint is that Realtors do not return their clients' calls.)

- How many clients do you currently have? Do you represent them to sell their home or help them buy a new home, or both? (If she has more than 10, pay close attention to the next question.)
- How often are you available to take me out to see new homes? (Will she be too busy to have time for you?)
- Are you strictly a buyer's agent, or do you list resales as well? (You want someone who works mainly for buyers only.)
- How many new-home sales have you negotiated? How many of these have closed escrow? (The more, the better.)
- Can I talk to three of your previous new-home buyers? (If she answered positively to the previous question, then she should be able to give you referrals.)
- How long have you been a Realtor? (Remember that new isn't always bad. A new agent who is dedicated will be a real asset with the help of this book.)
- Do you require a buyer's broker agreement? If so, how can it be terminated by either party? (A buyer's broker agreement is fine, but remember to negotiate a 90-day limit for commission payment after termination.)
- How do you search for new homes? (Does she have a computer program with a database of the new-home builders in your area? How can she find a deal for you that you can't find on your own?)
- How good are your negotiating skills? (You want someone who can be confrontational when needed, but still have some tact. Again, if she's new, she will gain the knowledge she needs from this book.)
- If I hire you, what would be my greatest benefit? (She will probably say service, and this is good. If she says she will save you money, then ask her how.)

The most important quality in a Realtor is to be able to trust her. Is she really going to read this book and follow the guidelines? Was she paying close attention to your questions and answering sincerely? Or did it sound like a usual sales pitch? A Realtor who is just starting out may have you for her only client. She will do everything to please you because you are all that she has. If you like her personality and you feel that you can really trust her, just make sure she reads this book and she will do great! We will be covering several techniques in this book that Realtors can and should do for you. When we talk about each subject for the first time, we will make a reference about Realtors so that you and your Realtor know that this is a Realtor duty. This will help you understand everything that the Realtor could do for you, if you decide to use one. It will also help your Realtor understand what is expected from her when she reads this book.

Chapter Summary

We have set some very strong demands on Realtors in this chapter. We have done this because we don't want you to get taken in by a fast-talking Realtor who only provides taxi service. We have seen Realtors who push their clients just because they want to make a deal. Insiders do not get pushed. Insiders are the ones in control.

We covered expected duties that Realtors can and should perform. We did this to educate Realtors on how to provide good service but also to let the taxi drivers know that you will not be interested in their service. We have asked a lot from Realtors, but just think of how much of an asset they will be for you when you find one who is willing to do everything.

Sometimes it is better to get a Realtor who is new to the profession. A new Realtor doesn't have the ego that inevitably comes with experience in this profession. She may be willing to learn more than a seasoned Realtor who may already think she's an expert just because she's "been around the block." Anyone who reads this book can be an expert. A Realtor with a great attitude and this book will be an awesome force in your search for a new home.

Finally, we want to say that it is completely up to you if you want to use a Realtor. You are going to be an Insider after finishing this book. You will have the knowledge to do everything needed to get a quality home built. You will know how to negotiate and what to negotiate for. We have simply told you how a Realtor can help and what a Realtor should do if you choose to use one.

Chapter 5

Advertising, The Art of Deception

In this chapter:

- The Media: Audio, Visual, and Print Advertisements
- Dissecting a False Ad
- The Bait and Switch
- Friendly Conversation, or Advertising?
- Transformational Vocabulary
- The Model Home Deception
- The Builder's Story
- Chapter Summary

Isn't it illegal to advertise something unless it is true? Actually it is, but it's also illegal to drive faster than the posted speed limit. Drive in the fast lane on any freeway in the country and you'll see just how often this law is broken. Unfortunately, the laws of advertising are broken, too, or at least bent just as often. We all seem to expect this deceit when we are shopping for a new car. But for some reason, we are much more trusting when it comes to shopping for a new home. If you are one of these trusting people, then you'll be taken advantage of almost every time.

We are going to put advertising under a microscope and show you what is real and what is false in an ad. Together we will dissect a false ad that was sent to thousands of people in the mail. Insiders discover the truth behind the ads and are aware of all the other marketing methods. There are several forms of advertising that builders use to promote their communities. You may be familiar with television, radio, and billboard ads, but there are several other forms of advertising that are not so easily recognized. Everything from the clothes a new-home agent wears to the vocabulary that she uses is directed at advertising the builder's product. Plus, the model homes are professionally designed and decorated to improve the image of the home. Did you know that even the furniture is specifically chosen for each individual model home to convey the proper feelings when you walk through it? It's all part of a manipulative process called the "critical path." This is the path that the new-home agent leads a prospective buyer, you, down to get you to buy a home. The marketing and advertisements are meant to start the buyer on that path. By the end of this chapter, you will be able to recognize the truth in ads, and then it will be you who will do the leading. As we have stated before, you are going to be an Insider, and Insiders never follow, they always lead.

The Media: Audio, Visual, and Print Advertisements

When new-home communities are promoted through the media, it's typically through three methods: (1) audio you hear on the radio; (2) visual you would see on the television; and (3) print you would see in magazine ads, mailed ads, or billboards. These advertisements are meant to accomplish one of two goals. They are meant to get you to either call or visit the community. A good ad will tell you just enough to peak your interest—you'll then want to find out more information, and to do that you must call or go in person to the community. A good media ad will never tell you everything that you want or need to know. If it did, you're likely not to visit or call the community, and if you don't come into the community, the builder won't be able to sell you a house. Ads are never meant to provide complete information. Actually, they're meant to hook you into coming into the community.

Let's use price as an example of how the builder will hook you into visiting their community. You might see an ad on a billboard or in the newspaper advertising floor plans starting at $139,900. In this ad, you might see a picture of a floor plan with four bedrooms and a three-car garage. Wow, looks good so far! Because this is the size of house that you are looking for, you might call or visit the community to see this house. If you decide to visit the community, then the ad has worked. You go there under the impression that you're going to see a four-bedroom house starting at $139,900. When you arrive, you are surprised to find out that the four-bedroom house in this particular community—the one pictured in the ad-actually starts at $159,900. What happened to the $139,900 home that you saw in the paper? That price was for the small three-bedroom house with a two-car garage. The floor plan is so small that the builder doesn't even build a model of it. In fact, the builder has sold very few, if any, of that particular model.

We have seen this trick used in several new-home communities. The builder never intended to sell any homes at the price of $139,900, but in order to advertise a starting price to hook people into coming in, they have to have at least one model they can say sells for that price. Once you are in the community, it's up to the new-home agent to get you interested in one of the more expensive models. You can save a trip by calling and asking what floor plan or size home is available for the base price of $139,900. You should also ask if they have that house modeled at the community. If the floor plan is the cheapest one in the community, the builder may not have it modeled because builders make bigger profits from the more expensive houses. Most buyers will not buy a home without seeing it modeled. If the builder shows only the more expensive houses, he is bound to sell more of these and make a bigger profit. At the same time, he can use the advertising hook of the low starting price for the community because he does offer the lower priced houses.

If you are using a Realtor, then she can weed out the phony ads for you. When you call the community for information about the ad you saw, you might need to be a little forceful with your questions. The new-home agent is not going to answer any more than she has to. She wants you to come into the community so that she can sell you a house. If she is good, she will give you only enough information to make you want to visit the community. We know several agents who will make up a story so they don't have to answer questions on the phone. The agent might tell you that she is in the middle of a contract and cannot talk right now. She may ask for your name and phone number so that she can call you back when she is free. Good agents will always want to establish a way to contact you if you don't come into the community so that they can follow up with you, a possible lead. A good agent might tell you that she is so busy with customers that she doesn't have time to answer your questions and that you really should come and see the houses yourself.

If the agent really is busy or in the middle of a contract, you can ask her for a good time to call back. If she balks at this, then tell her you are already preapproved for a loan and you are a serious buyer; you are interested in her community, but you must have a few questions answered before you come out and visit. This will let the agent know that you are serious, and if she is with a customer she will give you a time to call back. If she is just telling you a story, then she will answer your questions. There are communities where the agents are busy from the moment they open their doors. In this case, you might have to visit the community to get the answers that you need. We recommend trying to get the information over the phone before going to the community in person.

Another good and common hook that builders use are teaser-financing rates. An ad may offer a very low interest rate if you buy in their community. It goes something like this: If the going rate is 8% a year for a 30-year fixed rate, you might see an ad that offers 7.25% for a 30-year fixed rate loan. When you contact the community, you might discover that this rate is only good if you sign a contract within 48 hours. Or it might only be good for standing inventory homes that are already completed and will be delivered in 30 days or less. Unfortunately, some builders advertise these kinds of rates knowing they are completely false, just to hook you into coming to their community. We are going to dissect one of these ads in the next section. Before we do, we just want to make one thing perfectly clear—it is always better to call the community when you see something in an ad that appeals to you. This way, you can find out what the truth really is in an ad before you waste your time visiting the community.

Dissecting a False Ad

The ad that we are going to use was actually mailed to thousands of people in the Las Vegas, Nevada, area. We are not going to mention the real name of the builder here, and the picture of the home in the ad is left out, as well. We do need to mention that the picture in the ad was for the largest house in the community, with a base price of $189,900. The price quoted in the ad was from the low $140,000s, which reflected the starting price for the community. The builder wanted buyers to see an impressively large house in the picture and read "From the low 140,000s" right below the picture. This is another advertising ploy that builders use to give the impression of value—a much larger home for a much smaller price.

The written copy of the ad is where we are going to focus. The ad offers payments starting at $864 a month. It also offers a free washer, dryer, and refrigerator. The ad states the homes have up to five bedrooms with 2,900 square feet and 2 and 3 car garages. For only $864 a month, this sounds great, especially when you consider that the home is in a Master-planned Community.

Turn-Key Homes

By

Shady Builders

Payments starting at $864.00*
Located in Master-Planned Community
1,700–2,900 square feet
Up to 5 bedrooms & 3 baths
2 & 3 car garages

Free Washer, Dryer, and Refrigerator
With Every Turn-Key Home Purchase

*Monthly payment for principal and interest based on a sales price of $141,000 at 6.75% interest rate. Rates subject to change daily. Based on seller incentive of permanent rate buy-down on 30 yr. conventional fixed program.

In spite of our objections, the ad ran for one of the communities where we worked. Remember there was a picture of an impressive house above it, too. It appears to offer a pretty nice home for a very good price, but as we dissect the truth from this ad line by line, you will see how misleading it really is. Let's take a closer look at the ad.

We'll start with the title of the ad, "Turn-Key Homes." This builder uses the term *Turn-Key Homes* to describe the standing inventory homes in the community. These are homes that are already complete, and escrow can be closed within 30 days; notice the ad did not explain this time frame. This term actually eliminated half of the models we had in our community because we only had two models that were standing inventory at the time this ad was mailed out—neither of which were pictured in the ad. The next line states "Payments starting at $864.00." This is a great monthly payment for a new home in a Master-planned Community, but to understand this payment, you need to read the fine print at the bottom of the ad. We have enlarged the size of the fine print so we can read it without a magnifying glass. Notice the part that states "principal and interest" and that the payment is based on a "6.75% interest rate" with a "seller incentive of permanent rate buy-down on a 30 yr. conventional fixed program." First, principle and interest only, you may remember from chapter 2, does not include taxes, insurance, private mortgage insurance (PMI), or (HOA) dues. In this Master-planned Community, there was also a monthly charge called a local improvement district (LID) assessment. You remember from chapter 3 that in Las Vegas and many different parts of the country there can be local improvement district or special improvement district fees assessed to new homeowners. The LID in this community was $54 a month. Assuming that we could get the interest rate of 6.75% stated in the ad, we can now get a more accurate picture of what the monthly payment will really be:

Principle and interest	$864
Homeowner's insurance	$30
Property tax	$117
Private mortgage ins.	$70
LID	$54
HOA dues	$29
Total payment	$1,164

Once you add the complete monthly payment, you come to a total of $1,164. That's $300 higher than what was advertised. Are you starting to feel a little mislead? You should, but if this isn't enough to ruffle your feathers, then listen to this! While the builder was printing this particular ad, the interest rates went up drastically. One week prior to the ad being mailed out, we pleaded with our boss not to send it because there was no way we could honor the 6.75% interest rate. The best that we could do was a 7.75% fixed rate. Remember the fine print in the ad that stated ". . . seller incentive of permanent rate buy-down on 30 yr. conventional fixed program"? This means the builder is going to buy down the interest rate as an incentive for the buyer. The big problem here is when the builder was creating this ad, the interest rates were 1% lower then when the ad was ready to be mailed. The builder was only able to buy down the interest rate .25%; that would have brought the rate down from 7% to 6.75% for a 30-year fixed loan. When the interest rates rose to 8% the builder was only able to buy the rate down to 7.75%. This meant the principal and interest payments would be $959 instead of $864. This would be an increase of approximately $96 a month.

This $96 is a bad enough discrepancy, but when you add this amount to the other charges not mentioned in the ad, the difference becomes $396 for a total monthly payment of $1,260. Now we see they are advertising a home with a payment of $864 a month, which actually costs $1,260 a month when you add everything in that is required. To add insult to injury, our boss decided not to honor the "Free Washer, Dryer, and Refrigerator," either. He determined after the ad went out that it would be too expensive to give them away. This type of deceptive advertising is exactly what we have always fought against in the new-home industry. Not all ads are this misleading, but we want you to be prepared for anything that you might hear or see. Insiders are able to dissect an ad and determine by a phone call what is true and what is not.

Our boss did not care that the ad was misleading. He explained that the only reason for the ad was to bring people into the community. Remember, the builder's focus is hooking buyers to come into the community. Because we could not honor the ad, we asked him what he wanted us to do if someone came in with the ad, wanting to buy the house with the monthly payment we had advertised. Unfortunately, his reply was all too common in the new-home industry. He simply told us that, if someone wanted the lower payment, we should try to switch them to another loan program such as 7/1 ARM. In reality, we were sending out an ad that we could not come close to honoring. The ad was going to bring people in to our community, and once they were there we would switch them to another program in order to get them to buy the house. This technique is called the *bait and switch*. Let's talk about this next.

The Bait and Switch

The *bait and switch* is a technique used in many types of sales in this country. Probably the most often recognized is the automobile industry. You'll see a great ad for a new truck you want. The price is about $4,000 less than you have found anywhere, so you immediately jump in your car and drive to the dealer to see it. The ad makes it sound great, but when you see the truck, you find out it doesn't have air-conditioning, a radio, or even floor mats. It is a plain color, and to get all of the extras that you really want, it will cost you about $4,000 more than the ad price. The *bait* is the cheap price quoted in the ad. It's meant to lure you into the dealer. The *switch* is made at the dealer to get you to buy the truck that costs $4,000 more than the one in the ad. This technique is used every day in our country and is prevalent in the new-home industry.

The new-home ad in the previous section used a cheap monthly payment as the bait to bring in customers, but there are several forms of bait that you will see in new-home ads. You might see an ad that offers in big print $5,000 in options included in the price of the home. When you get to the community, you find out that only two homes have these options included, and they both are located on terrible lots. Of course, they will offer several other homes on great lots without the included options.

Insider Tidbit:

For the builder (the seller), a good print ad does not give out any specific information about the homes or the community except what is necessary to get a potential buyer to visit the community. Ads are to hook you or bait you into coming into the community. You can save yourself a lot of time by calling first and finding out the real truth behind an ad.

Friendly Conversation, or Advertising?

If you have decided after reading an ad to call a community for information, then be ready to be aggressive with your questions. Remember, the agent doesn't want to give you information over the phone. Because you are an Insider, you will be able to get the questions answered before you visit the community. Assuming that you still have an interest in visiting the community, you need to be a little prepared for the conversation that you are about to have. In chapter 6, we are going to cover the new-home search and what happens in the model homes, but we want to mention a few advertising techniques here first.

When you are talking to a new-home agent, she will always be trying to get information about you because she wants to know if you are a real buyer or just a *Looky-loo.* She will do her best to have a friendly conversation with you to establish rapport, which is just another word for control. A good new-home agent will also be dressed according to the price of the homes. She would never overdress in a lower priced community and never be under-dressed in a higher priced community. Her goal is to make you feel comfortable around her.

Her conversation will always seem friendly, but it will always be directed at selling you a house. Everything that she says will some-how compliment her community or be an attempt to win your confidence and trust. It may seem like she is interested in you, your life, and your family, but she is really categorizing your needs and desires in order to sell the house she wants you to buy. The new-home agent is trying to find out what you're looking for, what is on your "Needs and Wants List," plus what your hot buttons are. When she knows these, she can use a sales technique that highlights the features, at-tributes, and benefits, or FAB, of the house. FAB has been described many ways, but it always means the same thing. The agent knows what to say to make the house appear perfect to you because she will only highlight the FAB that fits your circumstances.

It's really slick when you think about it. You're having a ca-sual "How do you do" conversation, and actually she's creating a great list of information about you. You end up walking though the model with her, and you love the "feel" of it. She may high-light the feature of an in-home office and say the benefit is that you may choose to work at home. She points out the separate family room and kid's playroom and explains how your office will keep nice and quiet for you. She shows you a great storage closet, saying it would be a great space for kid's toys and camping gear.

Think back to that casual conversation you started when you walked into the new-home agent's office. Somewhere, you proba-bly mentioned that you had two kids, liked the outdoors, and you or your spouse works on the other side of town. Amazing how she focused on the specific features of that model to "fit" your family. But the reality of this model house that you "love the feel of," is that it's much bigger than you really need or want to afford. She's selling you the house she wants you to buy based on how she states how the houses' FAB fits some of your wants. Be very careful you don't get manipulated into something you don't want.

Insiders never trust a new-home agent. If they can gain your trust, it will be much easier for them to accomplish their goal. You must always remember that a new-home agent's goal is to sell all the houses in the community while getting the builder the best deal possible.

Transformational Vocabulary

Another technique the new-home agent uses in describing her community and the houses is called *transformational vocabulary*. It's actually an advertising technique that will change a negative feature about a house into a positive feature. If it is used correctly, it can make almost any house desirable regardless of the floor plan or where it is located. Table 5.1 gives a few examples of how an agent will describe her new-home community. A good agent will always use the terms in the "Right" column and not the "Wrong."

The examples in Table 5.1 are just some of the vocabulary that you will hear, but any feature about a house or a neighborhood can be changed to make it sound more positive. When you are looking at homes and talking to new-home agents, just remember to really look at a feature of a house to see what it really is. You may think that you would never fall for transformational vocabulary, but let us share a true story with you so that you can see just how easy it works.

Table 5.1   Example of Transformational Vocabulary

Wrong	Right
Tract	Community
Standard features	Included features
Lot	Home site
Sales agent	New-home counselor
Adding options	Customizing your home
Small backyard	Easy maintenance yard
Steep backyard grade	Landscaping opportunity
Standard oak cabinets	Picture-frame oak cabinets
Formica countertops	Solid-surface countertops

On one community that Jeff went to work at, there was a whole row of houses that were not selling nearly as well as the rest of the community. These houses were priced the same, and there was only one difference between them and the rest of the community—this row of houses backed up to a concrete wash instead of someone else's yard. When people learned that there would be a wash behind their house, they did not want the lot. No one wanted to buy a house that backed up to a wash. To turn sales around, Jeff used transformational vocabulary. He suggested that his partner stop using the word "wash" and start advertising the homes as "privacy home sites." At first his partner balked at the idea until she saw the first presentation that explained the benefits of buying a privacy home site.

Before people would even ask about this particular row of homes, Jeff would tell them he had privacy home sites available if they were interested. Homeowners are always interested in privacy, so of course everyone would ask about them. Jeff would then point out that this particular row of houses did not have neighbors behind it. The regular home sites would have someone behind each home so that your neighbors could see into your yard. We developed these particular homes so that the homeowner could have the privacy of not having another neighbor look into their yard. We were able to do this by building along a water passage. This guarantees that the homeowner will always have at least 25 feet of empty space behind his home.

After using this description of privacy home sites built along a water passage, the homes in this row went from the worst selling to one of the most popular sections of the community. Three people (two of whom were Realtors) even asked if there was a premium for these lots and were thrilled to find out that there wasn't. As an Insider, you are not going to be fooled by transformational vocabulary. You must see a neighborhood and a model home for what it really is and not what it is made to look like.

The Model Home Deception

Model homes are professionally designed and decorated to make the house look as desirable as it can possibly be. It seems obvious that a builder would want the home to look great, but the designing process goes beyond just nice furnishings. Much of the furniture that you will see in model homes was purchased to fit into that home only. Take a good look at the couch in the living room. Is it really big enough to fit your family? A common trick is to put a very small couch in the living room to make it look bigger. The same ploy is used in bedrooms if they are small. You may have a king-sized bed and like a certain model home. The bedroom in the model home that you are looking at may look big only because the model displays a double-sized bed. Another furniture illusion is the dining-room table. Many times there will be a beautifully decorated dining table that looks great. The problem is that it isn't really big enough to accommodate your family. Or the room may not be big enough to walk through with people sitting at the table. You need to take a good look at all of the furniture in each room and sit on it if you have to but make sure it is a realistic size. If you have specific furniture you want to accommodate in your new home, be sure to measure the model home to see if the furniture will fit in the rooms.

When you walk through the models, you will see several features that may or may not be identified as options. Sometimes near the front door there will be a list of options that are displayed in the home. This list will also state decorator items. Decorator items are furnishings such as wall mirrors that make the room look bigger. Typically, decorator items are not for sale and are only there to enhance the appearance of the model home. It's important for you to realize that the home you will buy will not have these decorator items. You also need to understand what the optional features and standard features are. You can have the new-home agent point out everything to you when you have her demonstrate the model. Insiders always have everything explained in a new-home model so that there is no question as to what is included and what is extra. In chapter 6, we are going to go on a sample tour of a model home. We will demonstrate how an Insider takes control from the start and learns everything that he needs to know.

The Builder's Story

Every builder will have a story about how they got started and what their mission is in building new homes. This story is written by advertising professionals and is meant to provide information for your benefit so you will be comfortable with hiring the builder to build you a home. What the builder really wants is to gain your trust and confidence. Some of the information in the builder's story may be true, but much of it could be false as well. We have seen builders advertise 30 years of experience when they have really only been in business for five years. The 30 years is claimed because they bought out companies that had been building for 25 years at the time of the purchase. Every builder advertises quality and service, but every builder also forces you to sign a contract that doesn't require them to finish the home. We will cover contracts in depth in chapter 8 and have no worries, because we are going to teach you how to make sure that your home is done before you move in. The simple point about the builder's story is that it may sound great, but it is basically an advertisement. It's the same as reading a magazine ad.

Chapter Summary

In this chapter, we have tried to point out how new-home communities advertise their product. We made the point that print ads are not to give out information but instead to bring you into their community. We showed you just how false an ad can be and together we dissected one of those ads.

One of the points of this chapter was to teach you how to read an ad and then know what questions to ask when you call the agent at the community. We want you to be aggressive on the phone and get the answers you need before visiting the community. If you are using a Realtor, she can do all of this for you before you go to look at the models.

We told you about FAB and transformational vocabulary and some of the phrases that you will hear on your model home tours. Insiders can distinguish between what sounds like a good feature and what really is a good feature.

When you are in the models, remember to take a close look at the furniture to see if it is realistic in size. Is the builder trying to make a very small living room look larger by using a love seat instead of a couch? You should take a measuring tape to make sure if you have any doubts about room sizes.

Finally, the builder's story will be presented in every model home office. A professional advertiser writes the builder's story, and you simply cannot trust everything that it states.

Chapter 6

The New-Home Search, Fun or Frustration?

In this chapter:

- The Model Home Greeting
- The Model Home Tour
- Puffing
- Finishing the Tour
- Using the Sales Office Questions
- Driving the Neighborhood
- Chapter Summary
- Sales Office Questions

We are now ready to start the search for your new home. The first five chapters have taught you how to determine what you want in a home and how to determine approximately where you want to live. We have also talked about the pros and cons of using a Realtor. If you do have a Realtor, then she should take an active part in everything that we discuss in this chapter. By now, you or your Realtor should have picked out several communities that appear to satisfy the checklists that you have created in the previous chapters. If you have taken these first steps, then your search will be much more fun than frustration.

Let's assume that it is going to be fun, and you have picked out several new-home communities to visit. At the end of this chapter, there is a list of questions, "Sales Office Questions," to ask the builder's agent when you visit the model homes. Some of these questions will put the agent on the spot, but she will quickly learn respect for you, and this will help insure honest answers. You are going to want to know as much about the builder as possible before buying the home. The builder's agent is going to want to answer as few questions as possible and learn as much as she can about you. There are some builder's agents that are just not very good at what they do. Like any profession, there are average agents and there are masters. This book is written to prepare you for the masters. Insiders can handle any agent's sales techniques because they know how the game is played. If you never let your guard down and treat every agent as a master, then you will win every time.

As you visit different communities, there are two impressions that we want you to leave with the builder's agents that you talk to. The first is that we want them to realize that you are very knowledgeable about the new-home industry. When an agent knows how smart you are, she will do a lot less exaggerating about her homes and will be a lot more honest. You want her to understand without a doubt that you will always require her to be able to back up her statements.

The second impression you want to leave is that you are a Crawler. We'll be using this term in later chapters, but for now just know that builders hate Crawlers. Crawlers force them to do the job right the first time. A Crawler projects a visual image of someone who gets down on his hands and knees and crawls under cabinets to see if anything was missed or built incorrectly, and this isn't far off from the truth. Crawlers are meticulous and demand everything to be perfect. We will be covering all of the steps to make you the best Crawler in the world; the first step in that process is to leave this impression with the new-home agent that you see in the sales office. When you choose the community and the builder that will build your home, you want to have their respect—everything you learn here will ensure you gain that respect.

In chapter 5, we covered many of the advertising techniques that builders use. We also talked about transformational vocabulary and how negative features will be described to appear as positive features. You remember that ads are not meant to give out information and are only there to get you into the sales office. You must now understand that builder's agents are not there to give out information either. They are there to sell the houses and write contracts. From the moment you walk into a sales office, a good agent will start prequalifying you and trying to close the sale. But that is okay because you have two new-home agents with you, and we are going to make sure that you get a quality built home for the best possible price. Now the strategy game begins.

In this chapter, we "walk through" a new-home community. You may have already visited many new-home communities and, if you have, you might recognize some of the phrases that are explained in this chapter. We give a real example and explain step-by-step what happens when you visit a model in a new-home community. We want you to know why certain questions are asked by the new-home agent and what she is trying to accomplish. We also want you to know what questions, sales office questions, you need to ask and just how to ask them. We felt the best way to explain this was to go through a complete model home tour.

When you walk into a sales office, you will notice that in most cases you will be in the garage of one of the models. Sometimes the office will be inside of the model or in some communities there will be a completely different building for the sales office. Whichever is the case, you typically see floor plans, a topo-board showing the houses in the community, and a professionally decorated office to make you feel comfortable. Our imaginary tour of a sales office and a model house is located in a town called Jackson. Because most of the sales offices are in the garage of one of the models, this is where our tour will start today. The players in this scenario are the new-home agent named Shelly and the buyer who will be you. Actually, you are a married couple, and we use the man and woman terminology to clarify the scenario and explanations. As we go through our tour, we pause in different parts with a detailed *(explanation)* so you understand what is happening and why; this way you will understand the complete process.

The Model Home Greeting

Scenario: You are driving up to a community you've selected called "Serenity Homes." The first thing you notice are the four models. The first model is where the sales office is located, in the garage of the house. You also notice there is a wrought iron fence surrounding all of the front yards of the models. The only way in or out of the model homes is through the sales office. You walk into the office and a professionally dressed friendly woman starts walking toward you with a big smile and says something like, "Hi, my name is Shelly, and what are your names?" As she is talking, she is reaching out her hand to shake yours and your wife's hand. You respond by telling her your name, and your wife does the same as you both shake her hand. The price of the homes that you are looking at will determine how Shelly is dressed and the vocabulary that she uses. For lower priced homes, Shelly will be in a nice casual but professional outfit. If these homes are in the higher priced range, she will be in a very expensive dress or suit with her hair done professionally. Serenity Homes are priced in the $150,000 range.

Explanation: The first thing an agent wants to do is establish rapport with you. Rapport is a warm and fuzzy word for control. The builder's agent will want to be in control at all times. This is how an agent can lead a prospective buyer into a sale. It is very important for Shelly to establish rapport with you as soon as you walk in the door. That's the reason for the friendly smile and handshake. A good agent goes far beyond this initial step. A good agent will be able to change the way you feel about her simply by what she says to you.

For example, when we greeted a couple coming into our office on a Sunday during football season, we might look seriously at the man and say, "We really appreciate you coming in today. It really makes us feel special; after all, it is Sunday and you could be home watching football, but instead you are here spending time with us." We would then smile, which would always bring on a bit of laughter or at least a smile from both the man and the woman. This simple exchange made a connection with the man. To the man, we were not just sales agents now but real people who understood how much he was sacrificing by missing his football games. The buyer could now relate to us on a more comfortable playing field. This is establishing rapport.

If a couple came in with an infant, we had another approach. Let's say the year is 2001 and the month is June. When the couple came in with an infant, we would look inquisitively at the child and say, "Well let's see, do we have a 2001 model here?" This simple comment would almost always bring a laugh and again would break the ice. For just a moment, we were no longer sales agents but warm-hearted people who cared about children; again, we established rapport.

A good builder's agent will always be able to make you feel good about something. If the agent can get you talking about something you love, it will make you feel good as well. Buying a new home is an emotional experience, and the good agent will want you feeling happy emotions as long as you are at her community. If you find yourself talking about something that makes you feel good but has nothing to do with buying a new home, then the agent may have just gained control. When you are feeling great, it is much easier to get information from you and lead you into an eventual purchase of a home.

Scenario: Back to our tour. After establishing rapport, Shelly's next question might be, "How did you find us today?" You tell her that you are looking for a home in this price range and you saw the Sunday newspaper ad. She says "great" and asks, "How long have you lived in the area?" You say you just moved to town. Shelly may then ask you, "What made you move to Jackson?" You reply by saying a job transfer. Shelly immediately responds with, "How wonderful, what is it that you do?" You tell her that you are with the electric company and that you have worked for them for seven years. Shelly will next ask your wife, "Are you enjoying Jackson?" . . . "What type of work do you do?" Your wife answers by saying she will be teaching at the elementary school.

Explanation: The greeting in the previous paragraphs takes about two minutes to accomplish. It is called "prequalifying the buyer." Shelly really couldn't care less why you came to Jackson or how much you like the city. All she wants to know is if you have been gainfully employed long enough to qualify for a home loan. She also wants to know approximately how much you and your wife earn, to ensure that you will be able to afford the monthly payment for the average loan in her community. In this scenario, you have given her the information that she wanted. You have been at your job for seven years and your wife is working as a teacher for the school district. Shelly knows from experience that the electric company and school district pay salaries high enough to qualify a buyer for a home loan in her community. New-home agents need to find out three things about prospective buyers. Are they "ready, willing, and able?" So far, Shelly thinks that you are "able" and she will now move on to the next step.

Scenario: Shelly will ask you something like, "In a perfect world, when would you like to move into your new home, and how many bedrooms do you think you will need?" You answer, "In about six months and we need four bedrooms." Shelly will quickly respond with, "Oh, why six months? Do you have a house to sell, or are you tied up in a lease?" You reply, "No, we can move at any time, but we just want to have time to look around." If Shelly has any standing inventory homes, she will become excited at this point. She tells you, "That's great. You are so lucky that you can move into a home at any time." Shelly will then say something like, "I have two absolutely gorgeous homes that will be ready in 30 days. These homes were both purchased, but the buyers could not complete the transaction. And what is really great is that both of these homes have four bedrooms, isn't that what you wanted?" Shelly knows that you will say yes to this question because you have already told her that you wanted four bedrooms. A good agent will never ask you a question that you can say no to unless it promotes the sale of the home. Shelly continues, "The builder will make a great deal on one of these homes, and only people like you are lucky enough to be in this position." Shelly may say that these two homes just became available and she has already had several interested buyers. She is trying to convince you that this opportunity is a one-time great deal, but you have to act fast.

Explanation: You remember from chapter 5 that standing inventory homes are houses that for one reason or another were completed before being sold. The buyers may not have completed the deal, or they just never sold because of some reason like a bad location or an unpopular floor plan. Whatever the reason, the builder wants to sell these houses because they are digging into his profit. Shelly wants to sell them because the builder is pressuring her, but also because they can close in 30 days and that is when she will get paid. When Shelly is telling you how lucky you are, she is really talking about herself because it is hard to find qualified buyers that can move into a new home in only 30 days. Shelly wants to convince you that you will get a great deal so that you will buy the home.

Shelly also wants to create a sense of urgency. She wants to make you feel that if you don't take advantage of this deal today, you are missing the chance of a lifetime. Insiders know that no matter how great the deal appears to be, there will always be another one tomorrow. Insiders never get caught up in the false sense of urgency that is created by new-home agents. You are not going to get caught up in that game either, and so you will politely tell Shelly that right now you would rather see the model homes.

Scenario: Shelly's next move is to get you registered in the community. Builder's agents do this by having you fill out registration cards. Shelly will say, "I would be happy to get you a brochure with floor plans while you fill out our guest card." A good agent will not ask you to fill out a registration card. *(Remember transformational vocabulary.)* She will just instruct you to fill out a guest card. A guest card sounds much less threatening than a registration card. It is easier to get a card filled out if you offer something in return, such as a brochure. It is also much more effective if you just instruct the buyer to fill out the card rather than asking him if he will.

Explanation: There are several ways to get registration cards from prospective buyers. Giving something in return for the card works very well in most circumstances. Agents can use very creative techniques to obtain cards, and we did in our offices as well. One of our favorite techniques was to hold a drawing for a free give-away. We have given away everything from a $250.00 shopping spree in the mall to an all expenses paid vacation to Hawaii. Getting accurate information on the cards is important if they are to be of any future use, and everyone will give their correct address and phone number for a chance to win a trip to Hawaii.

The registration card is a tracking tool for the builder and agent. The builder wants to know how many people are coming to his community. The cards ask for information about you, the visitor, such as income levels, what size of a house you are looking for, and what advertisement you saw. This helps the builder know if he is getting the right kind of buyer coming through his door for his community. It also helps the agent to follow up with you after you leave the community. The information you put on the card will be transferred into a database, and you will likely get letters and/or phone calls in the future to find out if the builder can still interest you in one of his houses. It is for this reason we recommend only filling out registration cards after you have seen the model homes and are genuinely interested in the community. The exception is for Realtors; you should always register your clients on the first visit to protect your representation of them.

Scenario: Back to our scenario. Declining to fill out the guest card is very easy. You just tell Shelly that you would rather see the models first and if you are interested at that point then you will be happy to fill out a card. Shelly might be persistent because agents are taught to get registration cards on everyone they can. She may even be reluctant to give you a brochure and price list without a card, but this is easy to overcome. Simply tell Shelly, "No, I really don't want to fill out a card at this time, but I do need a complete brochure to include prices and floor plans. Also, would you be kind enough to take us on a tour through the models?" At this statement, Shelly will forget all about the registration cards. Shelly is trying to create rapport, and the last thing she will want to do is get into a confrontation about the cards. Shelly also wants very much to demonstrate the home. Agents are taught that the more time they spend with the client, then the more sales they will make. They also know that they cannot control the situation unless they are with you. Because you have invited her to tour the models with you, she now thinks that she can gain control.

Insider Tidbit:

Insiders are always in control. Insiders want builder's agents to demonstrate the models because as an Insider you will have certain questions that need to be answered.

You may want Shelly to accompany you through all the models, or just one of them. You should have her go with you through at least one model because you will have questions that need to be answered. You will be leading the agent, and you will be getting the true information that you need to determine if this builder will meet your standards.

The Model Home Tour

As you leave the sales office and start toward the first model, stop Shelly in the front yard and ask her to explain what is included in the standard landscaping. The models will always be upgraded to look wonderful. Ask Shelly for a sketch of the front-yard landscaping if it is included with the home. You must also make sure that Shelly understands that you want her to point out all of the outside upgrades as well as the upgrades on the inside of the house. Some of these upgrades might be a covered porch, the type of front door, or coach lights next to the garage door. If you don't ask, Shelly will try to bypass some of the upgrades if there are several in the house. It sounds terrible to keep repeating, "this is an upgrade," because pretty soon it seems like everything in the house will cost you more and nothing is included. Remember, it's very important for Shelly to be making you feel good. If you start to think that everything in the house is extra, you will not be feeling good at all. She will always try to divert your attention away from a poor feature of a home and direct your attention toward a good feature of a home. *(Remember FAB.)* Shelly already knows what features are popular in her models and what features to stay away from. You want to make sure that you see the whole house slowly and notice everything. Ask every question that comes to mind.

When Shelly takes you through the front door, she will try to lead you to a corner of the room that makes the room appear much larger than it is. You should walk to every part of the room and view it from all sides. Notice the size of the furniture. Is it realistic, or is it made to make the room look bigger in the model? Shelly will have a set presentation and technique to demonstrate the features in the house. Look and see a feature through your own eyes, and don't let her vocabulary sway you. Use your checklist that you created in chapter 1 and make notes. You will be looking at several homes, and if you don't write down the answers to your questions and check to ensure the house covers your needs and wants, you will forget what you learned and saw at each community.

While Shelly is showing you the model, she will continue qualifying you and closing on the sale. She will be asking questions about your children or hobbies and interests. She will ask where you and your wife drive to work. She might ask if you plan to have more children in the future. Shelly will also want to know how long you plan to live in your new home. Remember that 7/1 ARM loan program from chapter 2 with the great interest rate? She might be able to sell you on that program if you only plan to live in the home for five or six years. Everything that Shelly will be asking you is for information to help her close on the sale. It is easy to think that you are having a casual conversation, but trust us, it is never casual.

Let's continue with our tour. Shelly asks, "Do you need a three-car garage, or would a two-car work just as well?" You reply by saying, "We have to have a three-car garage. I own a Harley Davidson, and it must be kept inside." Shelly enthusiastically responds, "Oh really, my brother owns a Harley and he treats that motorcycle like one of his children. I agree that you definitely need a three-car garage. What type of Harley do you have, and how long have you owned it?" You answer Shelly's question and proceed to talk about your bike.

Explanation: Shelly has just found something that you love and could talk about for days. Does Shelly really care what kind of Harley you have? No, she may not even be able to spell Harley, but it is common knowledge that Harley owners really love their bikes. Shelly wants you to feel good and start talking about something that will make you feel that way. If Shelly can get you and your wife talking about something that you love while walking through the model, then she's winning the game and in control. You may be talking about your Harley and feeling so good that you might miss the fact that the bedrooms are really small. You can leave that model feeling great and attaching that great feeling to the model and to Shelly. If Shelly is doing her job, then she will find something in common with you and your wife. She'll use that to establish rapport and get both of you talking about yourselves and feeling great. You must keep your mind on the model home and use your checklist.

In our scenario, we used a Harley Davidson motorcycle as an example to hook the man into feeling good and talking about something that he loved. We are not implying in any way that the builder's agent will try to influence the man first. Agents are taught to find out who the decision maker is within a couple and try to win that person over first. In our experience and according to statistics in research results, in over 70% of new-home purchases, it's the woman who makes the final decision to buy the home. Shelly may get a man talking about his Harley, but at the same time she will be paying very close attention to the woman's reaction in each room.

While Shelly is busy trying to get you both to feel good and overlook some of the disadvantages of this model, you will be asking several questions about the house and each room. Some of the questions you ask will be from your needs and wants list from chapter 1; others will be from the checklist at the end of this chapter. We know that we are giving you a bunch of checklists to read and use, but at the start of this book we promised to tell you everything that you needed to know to be an Insider. Consider using a clipboard or folder to organize your lists, and don't be afraid or shy to use them. They indicate that you mean business. Plus, all of these lists will guide you to finding your perfect dream home.

Scenario: Getting back to our model tour, you might ask Shelly, "How long has the builder been building homes in this area?" You should ask her, "Has the builder ever built under any other name?" You want to know how long the builder has built in the area because you don't want someone who is here today and gone tomorrow leaving you stuck with any problems that may arise. You also want to know if the builder has built under any other names because you will be researching the builder extensively in the next chapter. Using your checklists and any other questions that you can think of means you are leading the conversation— you want to be in control at all times. You should be discussing the house and/or the community while you are touring the model homes. If you find yourself getting off track, talking about "feeling good" subjects, go immediately back to your checklist and ask another question. Do not leave that model until all of your questions about it have been answered, and make sure that you write the answers down. Shelly will be a lot more careful about what she says if she sees that you are writing it down.

Puffing

Shelly may not have all the facts about a house or be able to answer all of your questions. If she doesn't think that you are paying that close of attention (*Remember the Harley.*), she may say something that is close to being right but a little exaggerated. This is called *puffing,* and it is legal. Puffing is actually a legal term in real estate. Puffing allows a real estate agent to exaggerate about a particular quality or feature of a home, but they cannot completely lie about it.

For example, you are looking at a home that has a nice game room, and you make a positive comment about it. Shelly immediately jumps in and says, "You are absolutely correct. This model is one of our most popular because of this great game room. A lot of people looking for new homes are concerned about resale value, and having this game room can make this house a lot more desirable for a future sale."

Now what exactly did Shelly say? It sounded like buying this home with the game room would increase the resale value, and that is exactly how it was meant to sound. Actually, she just hinted that it could be a desirable feature, or she "puffed up" the feature a little bit. Now if Shelly had said that having this game room guarantees more value on resale, then she could be guilty of deliberately being dishonest and she could lose her license. It is a fine line between the two. As you tour model homes you will hear a lot of puffing, but by taking notes you will be able to eliminate a lot of the dishonesty.

The builder's agent does have a fiduciary responsibility to be honest in all that she does. Lawyers have a legal obligation to be honest as well. Would you believe everything a lawyer tells you, especially if he was working for the other side? You must realize that anything the builder's agent says means nothing unless it is in writing. We will cover the contract extensively in chapter 8. By the time you get to that point with a builder, the new-home agent will know that she has to be completely honest and accurate when she is talking to you.

Sometimes an agent will not be sure about what is included in the model. This may sound unbelievable, but it happens quite often. If a community has just opened, then it is very possible that the builder hasn't decided what kind of features will be included in the homes. They may not even know what price to charge for several options that are displayed in the model. You may wonder who would buy a new home this way, but homes are sold this way every day. We have sold dozens of homes when we were not sure of what features would be included in the home. It's accomplished by building rapport with the buyer. Remember, another word for rapport is control. If Shelly can get you feeling good enough about your Harley or anything else, you will transfer that good feeling to her. It won't matter to you if everything isn't explained completely because you now like and trust Shelly. Trusting your builder's agent is like trusting an attorney for the opposing side of a lawsuit. We are not saying that new-home agents are bad people or dishonest. But you have to understand that the builder's agent is there to represent the builder. If she tries in anyway to work for or support you, she could lose her job and her real estate license.

Insider Tidbit:

Insiders would never buy a house unless they know exactly what is included in the home and its complete price. If the standard features and option list prices are not stated in writing, the builder's agent may try to be completely honest in what she "thinks" will be included in a house. After she has told you what she believes is an included feature, the builder might decide differently. Now you have to pay extra for what you thought was included. Insiders never allow any gray areas to exist in a new-home purchase. Gray areas will always go to the benefit of the builder. Insiders always get everything in writing.

Finishing the Tour

Once you have had a good look at the models, the next step is deciding if you are interested. If you have no interest in the homes you just saw, politely excuse yourself and thank the agent for her time. At this point, Shelly will start asking more questions as to why you didn't like the house. She is trying to figure out your objection so that she can overcome it and still sell you the house. Her efforts will be minimal because by now she knows that you are a very knowledgeable buyer and you know what you want. The checklist that you used in the model and the questions that you have asked convinced Shelly that you would not be an easy sale. But remember that Shelly could be a master, and masters pride themselves on overcoming objections and getting that tough sale. Shelly, being a master, wants to go into her next sales meeting and gloat over how she conquered this really tough buyer, so you may have to be polite but firm when leaving.

On the other hand, let's say that you liked the model, and you would like more information. More than likely, you'll be standing in the sales office after your model tour. Now is the time to finish the other questions from the sales office questions list that you didn't get covered while in the models.

You know, for example, from chapter 5 that the builder's story on the wall is advertisement and means nothing, and you want to know everything about the builder. You will want to question

Shelly about the builder's history. You may start by saying, "I have a few questions I'd like to ask you about your builder." Now proceed with whatever you missed like: "Who is the principle owner?" "Has the builder ever filed bankruptcy?" "Are there now, or have there ever been, any lawsuits against the builder?" "How many communities is the builder currently constructing in this city?" "Is the builder a member of the Better Business Bureau?" You will find all these questions on the list at the end of this chapter.

We also want you to ask Shelly, "If I buy a house here, will I receive a copy of the construction schedule?" "How often are there construction delays and for how long?" You should ask Shelly, "Will I be able to meet the superintendent?" You want Shelly to realize that you will be keeping a close eye on the construction process. You also want the superintendent to know that you will be watching as well. You want to become acquainted with the superintendent, or super, because he will ensure quality construction on your home. It is very important that the super knows he is building a home for humans and not just another closing. When it comes to adding that extra care or taking a little more time to do it right, the super who knows the family buying the house will always do it better. It is easy to let sloppy work go in a house for someone that the super will never meet. But it's difficult for anyone with a conscience to let poor construction take place on a house for someone that he knows. Now that you will be meeting the superintendent, you want Shelly to tell you what other communities he has worked on before coming here. This will help you when you start researching the builder in chapter 7.

While discussing the questions regarding construction, you will also want to know if there will be a *frame-walk*. A frame-walk is an inspection of the home after the framing stage of construction. The walk will take place right after the plumbing, electrical, and phone wires are installed. This inspection allows you to make sure all of the phone jacks, electrical outlets, and structural options have been installed correctly. It also provides another face-to-face meeting with the super. We have seen numerous mistakes discovered on frame-walks, even complete rooms missing or being constructed improperly. The framing stage is where you want to find mistakes because it is easy to go back and fix the problems. After the drywall has been installed, it can be very expensive to go in and tear out walls to fix an electrical or plumbing mistake.

Whether the builder has a frame-walk or not, you want to have access to the construction site. Make sure that Shelly has no problems with your visiting the site while your home is under construction. She will require you to wear a hard hat that she will have in the office: Wearing a hard hat is an OSHA requirement. OSHA (Office of Safety and Health Administration) is responsible for maintaining a safe work environment. The hard hats are to prevent injury from falling debris, and OSHA can fine builders if anyone is found on a construction site without a hat. This does not mean that you are restricted from visiting the site. Shelly will ask you to make sure that you do not interfere with the work crews because it will only slow them down. You will assure Shelly that you will not take over the construction process, but you do want to see the house being built.

By this time, after all your questions, Shelly figures you are "able and ready" to buy a house. Now she is doing her best to make you "willing" and is trying to get you into a contract on a house. She is trying to control the conversation by asking you questions that will give her buying signals. That is just fine because you will be an Insider by then, and Insiders are always in control. When you ask Shelly about videotaping, you will want to reiterate how important it is for you to be able to videotape the construction process. Shelly will probably say something like, "It is a wonderful idea, and videotaping is no problem at all." Now you want to add a little more meaning to the video camera. You tell Shelly that one of the reasons you want to videotape the construction is so you will have a record of just how well the house was built. If there were any defects in the wood or materials in the house, then the camera would pick it up. Having this record will be a great resale tool when you sell your house in the future.

If Shelly is working for a quality builder, she may be getting a little frustrated because she is not the one in control of the situation. However, she will keep trying to get control and continue to answer your questions. If she is working for a shoddy builder, then she will object to the video camera. She may come up with several excuses as to why cameras are not allowed. She may say that they will just get in the way of the construction crews. She might also say that the builder doesn't want his building techniques made public. These or any other excuses are groundless. If a builder does not want you to videotape the construction process, it is because he does not want you to see what he is doing. For whatever the reason, if a builder wants to hide his construction process, it can never be good. If this happens, you need to find another builder.

For our scenario, we will say that Shelly does work for a good builder. Although she is a little frustrated by not being in control of the conversation, she is gaining more respect for you by the minute. This is just what you want. You'll now add one more casual statement to the fact that you will be using a video camera. You will say, "Another good thing about the camera is that if there are any mistakes picked up on film, then we can get them fixed, right?" Of course Shelly will say yes: What else can she say? And you say, "Great, that is why I am going to hire a building inspector to monitor the construction process on site and review my films as well. Of course, he will not interfere with any of the construction crews. If he finds anything wrong, he will come to me and then I would come to you. Is that the best way to get corrections made?"

By now, Shelly is about ready to fall on the floor. She can't believe how thorough you are. She of course agrees that if you find anything wrong with the house that it will be immediately corrected. At this point, she will want to compliment you on being such a careful buyer and taking all of these steps to ensure that you will get a quality built home. That's what she is saying out loud, but in her mind she is thinking, "Oh boy, this buyer is going to be high maintenance." That is exactly what you want her to be thinking at this point.

When you have completed all of your questions and finished looking at the models that meet your standards, it is time to leave. It is fine to fill out the registration card at this point because you are truly interested in this community. You can tell Shelly that you like the community but that you need to do a little more research on the builder before you will be making a decision. You also need to visit a few other communities to see what they offer as well. Shelly will try to create urgency again by offering some reason for making a decision today, maybe by mentioning again the standing inventory homes she has. But you are an Insider, and you know that there will be another great deal tomorrow. You can divert this last attempt to sell you by asking Shelly, "Do you work a competitive floor with your partner? Because if you do, we will always make sure that we ask for you." After everything else that you have said, Shelly is now going to wonder if you have ever been a new-home agent.

The reason it's important to ask this question is because many builders staff their sales offices with what is called a *com-*

petitive floor. This means that the agents compete with each other for commissions. The commission is paid to the agent who makes the sale. Suppose Shelly had a partner, and she was working a competitive floor. She might have just spent two hours with you, and you may come back into the office on a day when she was off and buy a house. Her partner would get the commission, and in come communities Shelly would not be paid anything. In other situations, she may get half of the commission. Competitive floors are meant to create aggressive selling on the part of the agents. That's why an agent may seem pushy and try to keep you from walking out of the office. When you ask Shelly if she works a competitive floor, you are not only showing off your knowledge of the industry, but it makes her feel at ease because she will not lose a sale to her partner. This makes her feel good about you because you cared enough to ask. Remember, it is all about feeling good. See how simple a technique can be used to your advantage?

We do encourage you to be courteous and continue working with the new-home agent you started with; after all, you have established rapport with her. Remember, if it is a competitive floor, the agents have the same incentives to give away. One agent over another typically will not get you a better deal.

Using the Sales Office Questions

We have pretty much explained in the previous section when and where you might ask these questions. Here we wanted to provide you with a short synopsis of the "why" you would ask them. Plus, there are a few extra questions on this list that we did not specifically give examples for in the model home tour you just took. The questions on this list will not only provide you with a lot of necessary information, but they are convincing the builder's agent that you are going to be a Crawler and that she will have to be at her best every time she sees you. When you ask these questions, you can do it all at once, or you can break them up into different sections and ask them during different conversations, whatever makes you the most comfortable. But please, be sure you find out the answers.

1. *May I have a list of all included features, floor plans, and prices?*

    You want to have a complete brochure so that when you are at home looking and comparing it to other communities, it will help you remember what you have seen. You can put a copy of each checklist that you made with the brochure from each community.

2. *Do you have a list of available options and prices? What is your option policy?*

   It's nice to have a list of option prices because you can figure the total asking price of the home. You also want to know if the builder even offers the options that you want, and if not, you may have to make a nonstandard request. Some builders are reluctant to give you a complete option list; they don't want you to compare prices with other builders. On your first visit, it is not imperative to get an option list, but make sure that Shelly understands that you would never buy a house until you can look over all option costs. Plus, you want to know how much deposit the builder requires when ordering options and when the balance is due. By knowing these two items, you will be armed when you negotiate to buy a home. We'll discuss this further in chapter 8.

3. *Has the builder ever built new homes under any other name?*

   This question is important to help you research the builder's past. We have seen builders construct horrible new-home communities and simply change their name to avoid their bad reputation. Then they will go out and do the same thing again under a different name.

4. *Who is the principle owner?*

   This is another question for researching the builder. Some contractor boards ask for this information in order to give you their history. This question also tips off the builder's agent that you will be researching the builder thoroughly. She knows that she had better be correct in everything that she tells you.

5. *Has the builder ever filed bankruptcy?*

   It is very important that the builder be financially stable. You want to make sure that the builder is going to be able to finish your house without going out of business. If the builder has filed bankruptcy recently, within the last two years, then you will be looking that much harder at him when doing your research.

6. *Are there now, or have there ever been, any lawsuits against the builder?*

   The agent may not be able to answer this question because she doesn't know. If she is not sure, then you need to ask her to find the answer to this question and get back to you. If there are any lawsuits, you want to find out why. If the suits are over construction defects, then you may not want to consider this builder.

7. *How many communities is the builder currently constructing in this city?*

You are going to want to visit these communities when researching the builder. You also want to know that the builder is not going to just build this community and leave the state. If you run into problems after you move into your new home, you want to know that the builder is going to be around to take care of them.

8. *Is the builder a member of the Better Business Bureau?*

Being a member of the Better Business Bureau does not ensure an honest builder, but it does mean that he cannot have any outstanding complaints against him. You cannot become a member or stay a member of the Better Business Bureau unless you answer all complaints that are filed against you.

9. *Will I receive a copy of the construction schedule?*

Every builder has a construction schedule. It might say drywall in week 10 and cabinets in week 12. If you visit your house in week 10, you should see drywall being installed. If you don't then you know that your house might be delayed. Some builders will refuse to give you this schedule, but even if you can't get a copy of it, you are sending another strong signal that you will be watching closely.

10. *How often are there construction delays and for how long?*

Shelly will not want to answer this question, especially if the builder is always behind schedule. With these types of questions, though, you are telling the builder's agent that you are a Crawler. Be persistent and get an answer.

11. *Will I be able to meet the superintendent if I buy a house here?*

Meeting the superintendent allows you to establish a rapport with him. Plus, he will come to know you and see you as a person, taking the care in your house that he would for anyone he knows. You also want to know more about him, which will help you in your decision to buy in that neighborhood. We'll discuss this further in chapter 7.

12. *May I videotape the construction process?*

You want to be able to tape the process to ensure that the house is being constructed properly. It will also be a great sales aid when you want to resell your house. Imagine being able to tell a prospective buyer that a quality builder built your house and you have a videotape to prove it.

13. *Does the builder mind if I hire a home inspector?*

Shelly will always say no, and it is not up to the builder anyway. At this stage, it really isn't important if you hire one or not, but you want the builder's agent to think that you are.

14. *On average, how many items have been on punch lists at the walk-through?*

Now you are showing your knowledge of the building industry. A good answer would be 10 items or less. Shelly will always play this down. You will get the accurate amount when you research the builder, but you want to put her on the spot and get an answer from her now.

15. *Will the builder accept the Homebuyer's Protection Addendum (HPA)?*

Shelly will not know what you are talking about. You can give her a copy of the addendum or just simply tell her that it states you are allowed to keep money in escrow after the closing to motivate the builder to finish anything that is not done from the punch list. This addendum is to protect you from getting caught in the Closing Trap. If the builder's agent refuses to add the HPA, then ask why. After reading chapter 11, you will understand just how important this addendum is.

16. *Can I delay the closing until all punch list items have been done?*

Builders want you to close whether or not the punch list items have been addressed and/or repaired. That is why they will most likely not accept the HPA. Builders also want a smooth closing, and by asking this question you are sending a strong signal that you will be very difficult to close on unless the house is done perfectly. You will be reinforcing this feeling through out the building process. Shelly will likely fumble through some answer, trying to assure you that the house will be complete except for some minor items such as paint touch-ups.

17. *What warranty is included, and what exactly does it cover?*

    You want to know if the builder has just a one-year builder's warranty or if they also have purchased a 2-10 warranty. All builders will offer a one-year warranty, but if they purchase a 2-10 warranty, it gives you an extra year for plumbing and electrical, and an extra 9 years for foundation problems. You want the most warranty that you can get.

18. *What is the customer service procedure after closing?*

    Customer service is very important. If you need something fixed by the builder, you want to know that he will respond quickly. Do you have to mail in a service order, or can you fax or call it in? How long do they take to respond? You will be researching this question also with other homeowners.

19. *What would my total payment be with 5% down, to include all monthly costs such as taxes, insurance, HOA dues, etc.?*

    Almost all builders have computer programs that can print this information out for you in a couple of minutes. You have to make sure that all costs are included. Remember the false ad? Some programs are set up to include only part of the payment to make it sound more appealing. Insiders always get the complete payment. You can take this printout home and compare the total payments with other communities you're considering to help you make your decision.

20. *Are there any incentives offered to buy in this community?*

    Sometimes agents will tell you that they have 1% of the price of the home to give you if you buy in their community. Or, they may be giving away something else. Great! Now you know where to start negotiating. You will start your negotiating from the 1% incentive because you know that you can get that. In chapter 8, we will talk in depth about negotiations.

21. *Does it matter if we use your lender or our own?*

    All builders will have a preferred lender that they will want you to use. This is where being pre-approved by a competent lender works to your advantage. If you are not preapproved, Shelly will tell you that all incentives are based on using her lender. If you are preapproved by a good lender, then Shelly will not want to lose you, and she will tell you that it is okay to use your own lender.

Driving the Neighborhood

Before leaving the area, you want to drive the neighborhood. Remember in chapter 1 we suggested that you do this to consider different areas where you might want to live. If you have already driven two miles in each direction, then you may not need to do it again. We suggest that you do drive through again because you may have missed a few things on your first drive. Now that you are seriously considering this neighborhood, you want to take another look. You may have asked Shelly what the neighborhood is like, but she is not going to tell you anything that is bad. If there was a high crime rate, do you think that she would tell you? Shelly is not going to say anything bad about the community unless she is forced to do so. It's your responsibility to inspect the neighborhood and to learn as much about it as possible. You might want to review chapter 1 for aspects of a neighborhood that Insiders look for. As you drive through the neighborhood, always ask your family members how they would feel about living there. Once you have found a few communities that you like, it's time to research the builder, and we will do that in chapter 7.

Chapter Summary

In this chapter, we have taken you through the sales office and model so you know exactly what to expect from the new-home agent. We want you to know why she is asking the questions that she does because it's much easier for you to control the buying process when you know what the builder's agent is doing. As you continue to go through models, you will get better and better at asking your questions. There is nothing wrong with bringing out a list and a clipboard in front of the builder's agent. In fact, it is better for her to see that you have a complete list and that you are writing down her answers. Builder's agents will always be careful about what they say if you are writing it down.

We have given you a long list of sales office questions to ask, but we have explained why they are important as well. You will be spending several hours, or days, maybe even weeks finding your new home. You or your Realtor will be doing a lot of legwork, and sometimes it will seem tedious at best; but, this effort is for one of the biggest investments that you will make in your life. All of the work will be worth it to move into a well constructed home that will not give you any problems in the future.

Sales Office Questions

1. May I have a list of all included features, floor plans, and prices?
2. Do you have a list of available options and prices? What is your option policy?
3. Has the builder ever built new homes under any other name?
4. Who is the principle owner?
5. Has the builder ever filed bankruptcy?
6. Are there now, or have there ever been, any lawsuits against the builder?
7. How many communities is the builder currently constructing in this city?
8. Is the builder a member of the Better Business Bureau?
9. Will I receive a copy of the construction schedule?
10. How often are there construction delays and for how long?
11. Will I be able to meet the superintendent if I buy a house here?
12. May I videotape the construction process?
13. Does the builder mind if I hire a home inspector?
14. On average, how many items have been on punch lists at the walk-through?
15. Will the builder accept the Homebuyer's Protection Addendum (HPA)?
16. Can I delay the closing until all punch list items have been done?
17. What warranty is included, and what exactly does it cover?
18. What is the customer service procedure after closing?
19. What would my total payment be with 5% down, to include all monthly costs such as taxes, insurance, HOA dues, etc.?
20. Are there any incentives offered to buy in this community?
21. Does it matter if we use your lender or our own?

Chapter 7

Researching the Builder: This Is Serious!

In this chapter:

- Returning to the Community
- Visiting Homeowners
- Researching the Superintendent (Super)
- State Contractor's Board
- The Better Business Bureau (BBB)
- Chapter Summary
- Homeowner's Visit Checklist

After you have visited several new-home communities, you should be able to narrow down your list to just a few. When you have reached this point, it is time to research the builders on your list. If you are using a Realtor, then she can do everything in this chapter. Researching the builder takes a considerable amount of time, and this is one of the advantages of using a Realtor. You will start your research by returning to one of the new-home communities that you have selected. It would be nice to call first and ask for the same agent that you talked to earlier, making certain that she will be there when you arrive. Let's assume you are returning to the community where Shelly works.

Shelly will be thrilled that you asked for her and will look forward to seeing you again. She'll have a little bit of a mixed emotion because, on the one hand, she will be glad that you are returning to her community. This tells her you are genuinely interested in her community. On the other hand, she remembers how knowledgeable you are, and she knows she will have to be at her best to make a deal. Remember, Shelly is a master at making sales, so she is going to try to create urgency once again and sell you a home today. A lot of homes are purchased on the second visit to a community, and Shelly will feel confident that she will write a contract today. You will not be signing a contract today. That's just fine because you are an Insider and Insiders never sign a contract until they are completely satisfied and have all of the answers that they need. It will be at least your third visit to a community before you will be able to sign a contract.

In this chapter, we discuss what you need to know and what to ask about the builder. If Shelly is working for a good builder, she may be uncomfortable about answering your questions but she will still do it. If she is working for a bad builder, then you will meet with a lot of resistance. If Shelly refuses to cooperate with you in answering the questions from this chapter, you will be able to rule out this builder on the spot.

Returning to the Community

On your second visit to the community, you will be speaking with Shelly again. You want to do this because she has already developed a respect for you, and she knows you require correct answers. If you didn't get a chance to complete the Sales Office Questions from chapter 6, then you definitely want to complete it on this visit. Another piece of information you want to know is whether the builder is a publicly traded company. A publicly traded company has to report to stockholders, and this information will help you when you enter the negotiating phase. If the builder is a publicly traded company, then you also want to know the end of its fiscal year. This way you can figure out when its quarters end.

Every publicly traded company has to make quarterly and annual reports. These companies usually are willing to make better deals right before a quarter ends and especially before the end of the fiscal year. It will also make a difference when your home will be closing. Builders need to meet sales goals and closing goals. We will talk more about the closing in chapter 11. Shelly may be a little reluctant to give you this information, but we guarantee that she knows the answers to your questions. New-home agents are really pushed for sales and closings at the end of the quarter and the end of the fiscal year.

When you have all of your questions answered about the builder, you will need to make sure you know the name of the superintendent. You want to ask Shelly how long the super has worked on this community. After getting his name, you also want to know what community he came from: You will need this information in order to research the super. The person who has control of the building quality that goes into your house will be the superintendent. You must research this person as fully as you do the builder.

You should ask Shelly if you could meet the super at this time. She will probably say no and tell you that he doesn't have time to talk to every prospective buyer. This is true, but you never know. Some supers that we have worked with went out of their way to make the customer happy. If you do meet with the super, you can ask some of the same questions that you asked Shelly in chapter 6. Specifically, you'll ask if there are any construction delays and for how long? Ask him how many punch list items are usually on a walk-through? You can also ask him if he would be willing to do a frame-walk with you. It is nice to get these questions answered straight from the horse's mouth. But whether or not you get a chance to talk to the super, you will still get the answers to these questions from Shelly.

When you leave the office this time, Shelly should be a little less aggressive in trying to sell you a house, but she will still try. You have to be polite but firm and tell her you are still researching the builder. You then want to ask her for the location of the first phase and the current building phase in her community. She should be able to provide you with a simple map of the community and indicate on it where the phases are. You need to know this because you are going to visit both of these areas today.

Visiting Homeowners

We are going to start with the first phase that was built in the community. You will use the short "Homeowner's Visit Questions" list when you visit homeowners. It is short because you need to ask only a few questions of the homeowners themselves. It is also short because you want to be very considerate of people's time.

You should find, just as we did when we have knocked on doors or talked to homeowners, that they are very eager to talk about their homes. You will probably find yourself having to break away more often than having trouble getting people to talk to you.

If you see someone in his yard, it is very easy to go up and introduce yourself as a prospective neighbor. You simply say, "Hello, I am thinking about buying a home in this community, and I wonder if I might ask you a few questions?" You want to make sure that you are talking to the homeowner, and it is good to write down the address as well. That way you can always compare your records in the future, and if you ever wanted to go back to that same person, you would know where to go. As we did in chapter 6, we have a separate checklist at the end of this chapter for easy copying. Right now, let's go over each question and explain why it should be asked.

1. *How long have you lived here?*

   You want the homeowner to have lived there for at least 30 days. Any less time and they will not have been there long enough to come across many problems. If you are in a brand new community, they might have only been there a week, but the longer they have been there, the better.

2. *Was your house completed on time?*

   This is where you can compare his answers to what Shelly has told you. You want to hear the homeowner say that it was completed in the same month that was projected. If he tells you that the house was not done until three months after he was promised, ask him why. It might be because of something out of the builder's control, such as a shortage of building materials. Or it could be the builder is having financial difficulties. Delays can be caused because builders don't have the money to pay their subcontractors; when payments are delayed, the construction is delayed. Building incorrectly can also cause construction delays. Whatever the reason, you must find out why.

3. *How many punch list items were found on your walk-through?*

   Again, you will be able to compare his answer with what Shelly has told you. If he says he had about 10 items that needed to be done, then that is a good answer. If he says he had 20, 30, or more, then you need to be very suspect of this builder. You also need to be suspect of Shelly's answer if it differs from the homeowner's. The homeowner doesn't have any reason to lie, and his answers are usually the most credible.

4. *How long did it take the builder to fix the items found on your walk-through?*

This is very important because if he tells you that he still hasn't gotten everything fixed, then you know you have a builder with terrible customer service. Everything found on a walk-through should be completely done within 30 days of closing, at the very latest. The last thing that you want is to have a fight with a builder to get things on your walk-through list fixed.

5. *Have you had any problems with the house other than what was found on the walk-through?*

A brand new house that is built correctly should not have any problems popping up right after you move in. You want the home-owner to say that he has not had any problems except maybe getting a few of the walk-through items fixed. If he starts telling you about plumbing or electrical problems, then you just ruled out this builder. If he mentions one or two minor items that were fixed within 72 hours, then this builder can still be considered.

6. *How quickly were you able to get customer service to fix any problems?*

A good customer service section will respond within 48 to 72 hours, depending on the problem. A strong water leak is considered an emergency and will require immediate attention. If the homeowner tells you that he has to keep calling and bugging the builder to get anything done, then you can rule this builder out.

7. *Would you buy another home from this builder?*

This question will give you an overall impression of how this homeowner feels. If he says, "Yes, I definitely would buy another home," then you know he must have been happy overall with the home. If he tells you, "I would never buy another home from this builder," then you should ask him why. It may be obvious if all of the previous questions had negative answers.

Remember the "Rule of Three" and make sure that you talk to at least three homeowners. It would be better if you talked to five, but we cannot stress enough that you must talk to at least three. If you talk to one or two, then you might just get that one or two who are never pleased, no matter what. Or, they might be the only two that the builder did right. With at least three, you should get a good picture of the homeowner's satisfaction. If you get a mixed bag of answers, then you should keep interviewing more homeowners. You want to get the major impression of these homeowners, and you want that impression to match what Shelly has been telling you if you want to buy a home here. Once you have finished talking to the homeowners here, you will be going to the community where this superintendent last worked and asking several homeowners there the same questions. The more people you talk to, the better your research will be. You want to see a pattern develop of a home completed on time with very few walk-through items that were corrected within a couple of days of closing. Before you leave this community, you need to look at the current building phase. We'll now continue your research by looking more closely at the superintendent.

Researching the Superintendent (Super)

The questions on your homeowner's visit questions list were not only to research the builder but to research the superintendent as well. The super is in charge of all of the subcontractors (subs) on the site, and it's up to him to see that the construction is done correctly. We have seen great supers who stayed on top of their subs and completed a well constructed home with very minor problems at closing. Unfortunately, we have also seen other supers who couldn't care less about the quality of the homes constructed under their supervision. You should be aware that subcontractors are paid by the amount of jobs that they do. For instance, if a framer works on ten houses, then he gets paid for ten houses. If it takes him three days to do the job or six days to do it, he still gets paid the same. It's a lot more profitable for the framer to get the job done in three days because he will be getting paid more for his time. There is nothing wrong with getting the job done quickly as long as the job is done right. This is where the super comes into the picture. The super has a building schedule that he must stay on in order to meet closing deadlines. In a perfect world, all of the subs show up on time and do a good job while the super is watching over them to make sure of it. The builder is financially stable, and all of the materials arrive on time for each stage of construction. In our perfect world, our perfect builder is not concerned with deadlines because he is always on schedule. Also, he doesn't interfere, but allows the super to do his job and appreciates the job well done.

Now, let's talk about the real world. In the real world, superintendents are pushed everyday to get homes closed. Many builders even offer a bonus check to superintendents if they can exceed a certain number of closings in a month or a quarter. The faster a superintendent can get the job done, the better it is for the builder. They get paid when the house closes, not when it's sold. The rush to meet closing deadlines can put an enormous amount of pressure on the superintendent. He may want to do a good job, but deadlines will keep him from doing it. Rushing a house to get it completed is how many defects are created. Some of these defects may not show up for a year or two from the closing date, and that is conveniently after the warranty expires.

To show just how serious this pressure can be, we want to share a true story from one of the communities where Jeff worked. It was December, and approximately the 4th of the month. This particular builder had construction meetings on the first Monday of every month; that is common for many builders. In this meeting, they discussed which houses would close in that month and the date that they expected them to be closed. The homes that Jeff were selling took 13 weeks to build, from start to finish. Construction was behind in this particular community because of a late start on the current phase of construction.

The president of the company was at the meeting, along with the vice president of construction, the vice president of sales, the community's superintendent, Jeff, and his partner. One of the sold houses was in the fourth week of construction at the time of the meeting. The president looked at the vice president of construction and asked him, "Can't you get that home completed by the end of December?" He, in turn, looked at the superintendent and said, "You can get this home done, can't you?" The superintendent had two choices. One, he could have said, "Absolutely not, because this is only the fourth week of construction of a 13–week building schedule," and he would have lost his job. Two, he could say what he did: He agreed to finish the house by the end of December. Now the superintendent was suppose to cram nine weeks of building into four and do it over the Christmas holidays. Needless to say, the house was a mess when it closed, but it did close.

This story is a little extreme but not unusual, and unfortunately it is true. Good superintendents are forced to rush construction every day in the new-home industry. Put this pressure together with a bad superintendent, and the finished home will be a disaster. But if you have a good superintendent, he will be able to fight off most of the pressure from the builder and still build a quality home. This is the kind of superintendent that Insiders want working on their home. This is why you want to know where the superintendent was working before coming to the community that you are considering. Think about this when you talk to homeowners. You may be asking questions about the builder, but they are really about the superintendent and the builder.

You've finished interviewing the homeowners at your prospective community, and you understand the role the super plays on the construction site. Now you want to visit the current building phase at this community. If you visit during the week, you should see construction crews busy working. A phase may have anywhere from 6 to 10 or even 12 houses under construction. Typically, there will be several phases under construction at one time. For example, some may be in the framing stage, while others may be installing drywall.

Whatever phase they are in, it should be a very busy area. You may want to park your car out of the way and walk through the area before driving in the construction site because nails on the roads are a common hazard. When you walk down the road, look into the homes under construction. Are they littered with fast-food take-out bags? Is there a lot of trash lying around? We are not talking about construction materials; we are talking about cans or bottles and debris that should be put into trash cans. If this debris is not put into trash cans, it may end up in one of the drainpipes. We have had several new homes with plumbing problems because subcontractors threw their trash and debris down pipes rather than putting it in the trash cans. A good superintendent will demand that the construction site be kept clean. After purchasing a new home, you and/or your Realtor will be monitoring the building process very closely. At this stage, we just want to weed out any sloppy superintendents.

Insider Tidbit:

Insiders don't want plumbing problems after they move into their new home. It can take days and even weeks for trash and wood debris to swell up and block a drainpipe. Keeping a clean work site is the best way to prevent this problem.

State Contractor's Board

Not every state will have a state contractor's board. If your state does have a contractor's board, the purpose of the office is to monitor the work of contractors in the state. State laws do vary greatly, and we cannot give you every law for every state, but you should make yourself familiar with the office in your area. It is easy to call a contractor's board and ask questions. In several states, you can get information from the fax-on-demand service provided. Another great way to start researching the board is to use the Internet. The Internet is a great time-saver, especially if the contractor's board is not located in the city where you live. You may be able to get all of your questions answered just by using e-mail.

If the contractor's board is located close enough for you to pay a personal visit, then we recommend that you do so. It is always better to have a face-to-face with a human in an office than to be just another e-mail. When you visit the contractor's board, you want to ask the receptionist the following question, "How can I find out everything about a new-home builder?" Explain to her that you are buying a new home, and you want to do as much research as possible. The contractor's board will ask for the name of the builder or the name of the principle owner. It's a good idea to have both because then you can research not only the name of the current company but you can also research the owner's past. An owner might have built homes under another name and declared bankruptcy because of shoddy construction.

Your report from the contractor's board should tell you how many complaints were filed against the builder for a specific time period. Hopefully, you will get at least three years of history. It should also tell you how many complaints were considered valid by the contractor's board and how many were settled by the board. There may be complaints shown that the board did not consider valid. For example, the Nevada state contractor's board received 8,100 complaints of faulty workmanship over a five-year period from 1995 to 2000. Of those complaints, the board found 4,903 valid. Think about these numbers for a second. If there were 8,100 complaints filed over a five-year period, then that's about 30 complaints filed every week, and approximately 60%, or 18, of these were legitimate according to the board. You need to know if the builder you are researching is responsible for some of these complaints.

Your state contractor's board can provide you with a great deal of background information about any builder you are considering. Insiders always get this information before they buy from a builder. We have seen so many sad home buyers who are fighting with their builders to get things fixed. They are shocked when they discover that their builder has had several complaints filed against him with the contractor's board. They felt so sure that they could trust their builder. Why did they have that trust? Remember Shelly and the Harley? You are not going to be that trusting soul. You will be an Insider!

When you are at the board's office, ask the receptionist for all of the information about the board that you can receive. The board may have publications that you can have telling you the exact procedure to use in case you have to file a complaint. We don't want you to ever be in that position, but it might be helpful to let it slip out one day when talking to your new-home agent that you went to the board and are very knowledgeable in the board procedures. You can then ask her if she knows how many complaints have been filed against the builder. The agent won't know, but again you will be sending her a strong signal that you are going to be a Crawler.

You can also find out what kinds of complaints are most commonly found in the area where you live. This will help you during the construction process. If there are a lot of framing complaints at the contractor's board, then you will want to pay a little closer attention to the framing stage on your house. Another area of concern might be with soils complaints.

Here's another true example. There is an area in North Las Vegas called the "Golden Triangle" that has had numerous foundation subsidence problems. Subsidence occurs when homes were built on improper or expansive soils. Water and ground movement are leading causes for the soil to expand and/or shift. At the time of this writing, there are numerous lawsuits from homeowners living in that area against their builders, who were supposed to ensure that proper soil was used in the communities. Many of these homes are having serious foundation problems, and some are literally sinking into the ground. These homeowners would not have bought the homes if they had known about the problems in advance. To make matters worse, most if not all homeowner warranties do not cover subsidence. Insiders always take the time to do complete research before they buy.

When you visit the contractor's board, don't be surprised when you find out that you have to be a little persistent to get the answers and information that you need. Some boards are made up from the actual builders that they are supposed to regulate and monitor. The belief is that the best possible person to investigate a complaint against a builder would be another builder. Who else would be better qualified? This may be true, and in theory it might sound good too. But if the majority of the board is made up of active builders, it becomes a little difficult to hand out stiff fines for noncompliance of the laws for fear the same could be done to them. It's a little like fining themselves.

That is why you want to know everything about the board and just how they perform their responsibilities. If your contractor's board is made up of local builders, then you might figure they are very lenient toward other builders. If this is the case, then the complaints that are registered as valid have that much more importance. If you ever need to file a complaint with the board, it is much more likely to go in your favor if you know exactly what they will consider valid. You want to ask them if they will consider a videotape evidence of poor construction. They should. Your next question should be whether they will take action before you close on a home. Some contractor's boards will not take action until after the purchase is final. By then, your home is already complete, and to fix the defect, the builder may have to tear out walls to fix the problem. If the contractor's board will take action during the construction process, it will be another tool you can use to force the builder to do the job right the first time. Insiders use every resource to their advantage. The state contractor's board is a good resource to use, but it's not the only one.

The Better Business Bureau (BBB)

The Better Business Bureau (BBB) is another resource for you to use in researching a prospective builder. Again, you can call the office, but we suggest that you go in person. The BBB is not a government agency and has no authority to fine or discipline its members. It's an organization that is there to promote good business practices. This is an attempt by the business community at large to regulate itself. The BBB keeps files on every business owner in the local community that is a member of its organization. It also keeps files on business complaints. If a complaint is filed with them on one of their members, they will contact the member and send a copy of the complaint. This action will require the member to answer the complaint within a certain amount of time. A business cannot remain a member in good standing if it does not at least answer all complaints. If a complaint is filed against a business that is not a member, then the BBB will simply send a copy of the complaint to the business. It will keep a record of the complaints against nonmembers, but they have no way to compel the business owner to respond to the complaint.

The BBB has different programs for business owners. One such program that we were former members of is called the "We-Care Program." It guarantees that the member will submit to impartial arbitration if the business and customer cannot reach a settlement on their own. This program provides greater assurance of customer satisfaction because the business owner is promising to resolve all complaints to help satisfy his customer. But even a regular member who does not participate in the We-Care Program must have all complaints answered to remain a member. A business owner cannot become a member of the BBB with a list of complaints against them, either. If the builder that you are researching is a member of the BBB, you at least know that all complaints from home buyers have been answered. This doesn't mean that the home buyer got satisfaction with the answer; it just means an answer was received.

When you research a builder through the BBB, you will want to know the name of the builder and the principle owner, just as you did with the state contractor's board. If the principle owner had another business, you can research that as well. You can usually research up to three builders at a time with the BBB. They will give you a written report of the information they have on the business. In this report, complaints will be explained and what action, if any, the business owner took. The report will tell you if any complaints are outstanding. You do not want to buy a home from a builder who has outstanding complaints with the BBB, because if he does it means he is not responding to homeowners' complaints. One of the nice things about the written report is that it is usually very detailed. We have received reports that had pages of complaints against a business, and it described in detail what these complaints were.

The best scenario that you can discover about a builder you are researching is that he is a member of the BBB and takes part in the We-Care Program. That is, of course, if the We-Care Program is offered in the area where you live. The next-best scenario is that the builder is a BBB member with no complaints filed against him. The last but still acceptable scenario would be that the builder is not a BBB member, but has no complaints filed against him. If the builder you are researching has any outstanding complaints, or if he has had several complaints, then you might want to consider another builder.

Chapter Summary

In this chapter, we have taught you how an Insider researches a builder. You now know that it's not only the builder but also the superintendent that must be researched. We have seen new-home communities built with quality by good superintendents. We have also seen communities by the same builder built with faulty construction because of a superintendent that didn't care. You must know who your superintendent is and research his past and current projects.

We have talked about using the state contractor's board to find past information about your builder. Not only will this help you decide who is reliable, but it will also get you more respect from the builder when he knows you are familiar with the state board. It will also allow you to learn what kinds of construction problems are common in your area of the country. It will be much easier for you to spot mistakes if you know which ones are made more often.

You know how to use the Better Business Bureau to get more information on your builder. If the builder is a member in good standing, it's a plus for you. It adds a little more credibility to the builder to be a member in good standing, especially if he is a member of the We-Care Program. Most people know about the Better Business Bureau, and because of that recognition it is here that you might find the most complaints if there are any about a builder.

Finally, but more importantly, we gave you yet another checklist of questions to ask of the homeowners you visit. This is the most important research that you can do. Homeowners have no reason to lie, and they love to talk about their new homes. If you don't do any other research at all, make sure that you do this. We have told you to visit at least three homeowners at the community where you are considering buying and at least three more at the community where the superintendent previously worked.

ιe homeowners are to be understood as the minimum re-
ρed to get the information that you need. Just remember, the
more homeowners you can talk to, the better your research will
be. If you are using a Realtor, then she will love to go and do this
for you; this is where a Realtor could really pay off for you. There
is no dollar figure to attach to the inexpressible comfort of knowing that a quality builder is building your new home. The only
way to know and enjoy that feeling is to do the research.

Once you have the state contractor's board report, the Better
Business Bureau's report, and the answers that you have gotten
from homeowners, you will be in a great position to decide which
builders you would want to use. Add this information to your impression of the construction sites that you visited and your research of the superintendents and you can now make an
informed decision about the builder you choose to build your
home. The builder you choose must be able to pass all of these
tests. Now, you only have to pick out the model you like best before you move onto the next step—the negotiation.

Homeowner's Visit Questions

1. How long have you lived here?
2. Was you house completed on time?
3. How many punch list items were found on your walk-through?
4. How long did it take the builder to fix the items found on your walk-through?
5. Have you had any problems with the house other than what was found on the walk-through?
6. How quickly were you able to get customer service to fix any problems?
7. Would you buy another home from this builder?

Chapter 8

The Negotiation: Here Is Where You Win!

In this chapter:

- All about Options
- The First One to Name a Price Loses
- Negotiating for a 30-Day Close
- Negotiating for a Home Under Construction
- Negotiating for a Home That Has Not Been Started
- Techniques to Use in All Negotiations
- The Offer and Counteroffer
- The Contract
- Closing the Deal
- Chapter Summary

Once you have found the home of your choice and a reputable builder, you're ready to negotiate the purchase price. You may think that new-home prices are not negotiable, but they are. Remember, and never forget, that everything in real estate is negotiable. If you decided to use a Realtor, then she can do everything in this chapter for you. If you do not have a Realtor, then you will be the one negotiating. We always want you to be polite and courteous, but you must be firm and maybe a little confrontational as well. Don't feel that you must be as nice to the new-home agent as you would to a friend; the new-home agent is always working for the builder, no matter how nice she seems.

Insiders have the big advantage when it comes to negotiating for a new home. By the time you've reached this step in the buying process, the builder's agent knows you are an astute buyer. She knows that she will have to be at her best to get you into a contract. She's right: Even if you make up your mind to buy one of her houses, she won't realize that until you say, "Let's sign the contract." The negotiation is a battle of wits, and no one will be able to battle better than you. So let's take some time and explain the rules of engagement.

All about Options

We've dedicated a section to options because they are so much a part of the price of your home. In chapter 1, we talked about which options increase the value of resale as opposed to just making the home more salable. But, there is much more to learn about options and how they determine the final price of the home.

During your first visit, you should have asked about the builder's option policy; how much, if any, deposit is required when ordering options; and how you order them. A typical response will be that ordering options will be necessary before construction cutoff dates. A cutoff date is the point in construction when an option can no longer be added to the house. An example would be putting in a fireplace after the slab and framing have been started. A fireplace must be planned before the slab is poured. The date assigned for the slab to be poured would be the cutoff date for requesting a fireplace. The fireplace would have to be ordered and paid for before the slab-pouring date.

The builder's agent may also say to you, "You will need to pay a deposit of 50% of the option cost at the time you place your order." She may then say something like, "The builder requires this amount in order to pay for the upgraded materials." Some builders require a buyer to pay 100% of the cost for options at the time they are ordered. All builders want home buyers to buy as many options as possible and as soon as they can, and there is always some kind of deposit or payment in full. The reason for the rush is because option money is not refundable. Once the builder has your option money, he can feel confident that you won't back out of the deal. It will be the agent's job to get you to pay for options as soon as she can. Once she has your option money, it will be much easier for her to keep you under control.

There are two basic ways that you will purchase options from a builder. With the first, you select the options of your choice from a list the builder's agent has provided you before you signed the contract. The second way, which is becoming more popular with builders, is to send you to one of their design centers to buy your options. We want to explain how each system works and how an Insider would make either system work for him.

If you are buying your options from the builder's agent in the sales office, then most likely she is getting a small commission from the sale. She knows that if she can sell you more options, she will get a bigger commission. You also know the builder is making, on average, a 40% profit from every option that you buy. Insiders like to buy the options from the builder's agents because you will have all of the prices right there before you sign a contract. This way it is easier for you to compute the total price for the house and figure out what you are going to make as an offer.

Builder's agents will want you to buy the house first and then decide on how much you want to spend on your options. This means you would sign a contract to buy a home before you know the full price. Insiders never sign any contract until they know the full price—the house price plus the cost of all the options you want in it. Even if you decide not to purchase your options at the time you sign the contract, you still want to know how much they will cost you when you do decide to purchase them.

If you are buying a new home and you can't get any discounts from buying the options at the time of contract, then you may not want to pay for them until you get near the construction cutoff dates for each particular ordered option. There is no benefit to ordering the options early if it's not saving you money. The builder, on the other hand, wants you to order options as soon as possible. He may have a statement on his option list like "The prices are subject to change without notice" and only by purchasing the options do you "lock in" their prices.

This is a potential risk you should weigh for yourself: Keep your money until just before the options cutoff and maybe pay more for the option, or pay the deposit amount right away and lock in the option cost. Ask the builder's agent when was the last change in pricing or if she is aware of any coming up. She'll tell you the best she knows, but temper that with the fact that she wants you to buy your options as soon as possible. Remember, once you have ordered options and paid the deposit for them, your option money is nonrefundable. If for any reason you fall out of the deal, then you will not get your option money back. Getting a buyer to buy options on a new home is one solid way to lock the buyer into the deal for good. In the negotiation examples that follow, we show you how to use this technique to your advantage.

If you don't order your options from the builder's agent, then you will go to a design center. We have seen these centers set up to order everything for your house, including flooring and window coverings. Usually they will not cover structural changes; these you will probably request from the builder's agent at the sales office. The design centers are not staffed with real estate agents. They are staffed with sales representatives (reps), and their job is to sell you as many options that they think you can afford. These sales reps are paid a commission based on the amount that you spend, so you can expect to always be led to the most expensive choice on every option. Don't be surprised if you have to ask to see the complete line of prices for items such as countertops or flooring. Insiders decide what they want in their home and will not let fast-talking sales reps manipulate them into something more expensive that they really don't want. When you are in a design center, it's the same experience as in any other commission sales situation.

If you will be ordering options from a design center, then you'll likely have to be a little more forceful with the new-home agent to get an option price list. Builders want you to buy your home first and then make an appointment to see the design center's staff. They want to treat it separately, as if it was something extra and not part of the price of the home. Insiders know that the option price is very important to the total price of the home. You must insist on getting a price list of options before you sign any contract, even if the options are bought at a design center. Many buyers regrettably find out after they have signed a contract that the options they really wanted cost much more than they wanted to spend. Insiders never find out after the contract is signed. If Insiders can't get a list of option prices before they sign a contract, then there is no contract. Don't ever let the builder's agent talk you into signing a contract before you know all of the option prices.

Another reason to obtain an option list up front is to ensure that the builder offers the options/additions you want. If they do not and you decide to pursue a house there, you'll be asking for a nonstandard change from the builder to get the addition you want. A nonstandard change is any option that you want that is not on the builder's option list. Anything not on that list will have to be researched by the builder for a price.

For example, let's say that you want the master bedroom door built into an arch with a double-door entry and window above the door, but the builder doesn't offer this as an option. The builder will have to determine the cost of materials and then get a price on labor from the subcontractors who will perform the labor. The next step is to add approximately a 40% profit, and that will give them the final price of the nonstandard change they will charge you.

Insider Tidbit:

If the builder simply does not want to do your nonstandard request, then he will sometimes overinflate the price to discourage you from requesting it. We have seen prices quoted 200% above the cost, just because the builder or the superintendent did not want to do the nonstandard request. It's saying no with a price. If you accept their inflated price, their profit margin makes up for the inconvenience of the construction.

Sometimes Builders will discourage the requests by saying they will not research a price without a signed contract to buy and/or ask for a fee to cover staff research time. It may appear that they are being uncooperative and making it difficult to request nonstandard changes; that's probably an accurate assessment. If they are making it difficult, they most likely are trying to avoid doing any specialty requests, and that's not uncommon.

One more thing about option prices: Builders love to use options to negotiate a deal. A builder might offer you $5,000 in free options. This sounds like a lot, but remember that the builder is getting a 40% profit from those options, so he is really only spending $3,000. When a builder offers you a credit toward options, always ask for more; most of the time, you will get it.

The First One to Name a Price Loses

When you set out to negotiate a purchase price for your home, think of it as a game of chess. If we know what move you are about to make in a game of chess, then we will be able to counter it immediately. If we continue to know every move that you will make, then we will have you in checkmate in no time. It's the same concept when you negotiate a price on a new home. If you are the first one to offer a price, you will lose every time. You will lose because the builder's agent now knows what you are willing to pay for the home; you have tipped your hand, given away your move. She might have been able to accept a price much lower than the one you offered, but now it's too late.

Fortunately, when you are buying a new home, the price should be stated on the brochure. What is also fortunate is that many builders advertise incentives to entice you to purchase in their community. Some may have a 1% incentive to be used toward closing costs, or they may just give you a dollar figure up front that you can have to use for options. Before you even talk about a certain house, you want to ask if there are any incentives to buy in the community. Many inexperienced agents will tell you all of their incentives before you even say that you want to buy. This is great for you because you would then know everything that the builder is giving away before you even start your negotiations.

Whatever the builder offers to give you will be your starting point for negotiations. If the builder offers you 1% of the base price of the home to be used for closing costs, then you know the 1% is a "freebie," and you will start negotiating from there. The builder was the first one to name a price, so now when you're ready to make your move and negotiate for your home, you're in the position of control.

But let's not get ahead of ourselves; we need to remember that the base price of the home is only part of the complete price of the home. You may still want to purchase some upgrades. How will this affect the negotiations? You now know that any option you choose to add to your house will give the builder an additional 40% profit on top of the profit from the house itself (approximately 7%). When you negotiate the price of the house, you will want to negotiate the price of the options at the same time. This is a big reason why you have been making out your wants and needs lists for what you wanted in your home. You may have changed your list ten times in your new-home search, but by now you should have a good idea of what you really want in your home. It is also why we stated in chapter 6 that you would need a copy of their option list before you were ready to go to contract. You want to review their list and determine how much, if any, you would be adding to the base price of the home in option costs.

Builders want you to buy as many options as possible because that's where their biggest profits are. But for Insiders, it's also where your biggest savings are. You will always get a better deal if you can negotiate all of your options and the base price of the home at the same time. The savings you can get on any new home will depend not only on your negotiating skills but also on how far along the house is in the construction process. Because the negotiation process is very different, we are going to go through three scenarios to demonstrate different phases of construction. The negotiation techniques that you use will depend on how soon you want to move into your new home.

Negotiating for a 30-Day Close

If you need or just want to move into your new home within one month or less, then you will need to find a standing inventory home. This home is one that is completely built; typically, the floor covering is not installed. There are two kinds of standing inventory homes that you will see. The first is a home that was purchased by another buyer, and for some reason the deal could not be completed. Now the builder has a home that is finished and eating into his profit margin, because every month he has to make a payment to the bank as long as he owns the completed home.

The second type of standing inventory home is one that for one reason or another was just never purchased. The builder started the home with the belief that someone would buy it before it was completed. This type of home is called a *spec home;* it's built on the speculation that someone will buy it. It is extremely important for you to know which type of home it is that you are seeking. You need to know if the home was purchased before, because if it was, then the previous owner might have paid for the options that are in the house. Why should you pay for something that has already been paid for? Insiders never pay for options unless they have to, so we want you to use the following technique in the sales office.

Why don't we use Shelly again, because she has been so helpful in the past. When you come back into her community, she will know you by now, and you will have the house that you want picked out in your mind. You've decided to buy a standing inventory home, but you don't want Shelly to know this just yet. You will tell her that you are very interested in her community, but you wanted to find out how her option policy works. You have already asked her this question before, but it is good to confirm the answer now—plus you're throwing her off your track. You ask her, "If I buy a home, how soon after the purchase will I need to pick out options? And is there a deposit, or do they need to be paid in full at the time they are ordered?" She should tell you again what you learned during your research visit. For our scenario, we'll say that they must be ordered before the construction cutoff, and you must pay a 50% deposit when you purchase an option. Your next question for Shelly is, "When is the balance of the option payments due?" If Shelly tells you that they must be paid 30 days before closing, you now have very powerful negotiating information.

Here is how an Insider will use this knowledge to his advantage. Most likely, this conversation is taking place around the topo-board (map of the community), and you will see on this map the houses that are completed and under construction. You are focusing on the standing inventory homes in the model you like. Hopefully, during your research visit to this community you remembered to mark down the location of the different houses so you know ahead of time which house in particular you want. You can now casually ask Shelly why a certain house never sold. Actually, the house you point to is the one you want to buy, but you don't want her to know that just yet. If Shelly says that it did sell but the buyer "fell out," then you want to ask her when it fell out. A good way to ask is, "How long has it been sitting there?" You hope she says for only a couple of weeks. You know because of their option policy that if this house is completely finished and the buyer "fell out" only two weeks ago, all of the options in the house should have been paid for by the previous buyer. If there are $10,000 worth of options in that house, you might be able to get them for free. A builder is usually eager to sell the house, but he will also try to get paid twice for the same options. Insiders know better.

Let's use this house as an example and break down the numbers:

Base price of the home	$200,000
Upgrades in the home	10,000
Total price of the home	$210,000

Insiders know that builders make approximately 7% profit from the base price of each home and about 40% profit from options. In our example, if you paid the builder his asking price of

$210,000, he would make $14,000 profit from the base price and $4,000 profit from the options. But wait; remember, Shelly told you that this house was already purchased and the buyer fell out just before closing. In this case, the builder should have already been paid the $10,000 for the options. If you pay the full price for the home, you will be increasing the builder's profit from $18,000 to $28,000 because the options would have been purchased twice. Builders get paid twice for options every day in the new-home industry, but never from Insiders.

An Insider would not offer more than 195,000 for this home. Would a builder go for a $15,000 discount on a standing home like this? Yes, because the builder wants to sell standing inventory as soon as possible, and with your detective work you already know that he should have been paid for the options. So what would the builder really get paid with your offer?

Total price you pay	$195,000
Options paid for already	10,000
Total builder was paid	$205,000

Even though you save $15,000 on the purchase price of the new home, the builder still gets a good profit of $13,000—almost all of his original asking price for the home. He also gets to unload a standing inventory home that would have cost him money for every month it remained unsold.

See how much you can save with Insider information? A standing inventory home can be a tremendous deal if you approach it with the right technique. Do you think Shelly would have told you about the option policy if she had known that you were interested in a standing inventory home? Do you think that she would have told you that the buyers just fell out of the deal? Not if she was a good agent. Remember the chess game and knowing the other person's move in advance? Insiders never give away their next move until they know that they can get what they want.

You may not be able to buy a standing inventory home that was pre-owned. Let's say in the previous scenario that the home you decided to buy was a spec home, never bought before. We'll use the same numbers to show you how an Insider would approach this house. On a spec home, the options that were put into the home were most likely picked out by the new-home agent on site. She knows what options are the most popular, and she will put these into the house with the confidence that she will be able to sell them to a prospective buyer. Unfortunately for her and the builder, the house didn't sell and now is a part of the standing inventory. Even though the builder has not been paid anything for this house, he is very motivated to sell it because, as you know, standing inventory eats away at his profit margin.

The spec home has a base price of $200,000 and $10,000 worth of options for a total price of $210,000. The profit would be $18,000 if the builder gets the full purchase price for the home. If this house was still under construction and they could offer additional options to a buyer, the builder would be very confident of getting his full purchase price; but at this point he's in trouble. The home is finished, and no one has bought it. An Insider would make an offer of $199,000 to purchase this home—not paying for any options and getting a slight discount on the base price. This still allows the builder to make a nice profit on the home, and it allows you to get an $11,000 discount. Since you are a pre-approved buyer and willing to close in 30 days, it is very likely that the builder will accept this offer. Here again, you will save a lot of money because you know the builder's profit margin.

Now that we've analyzed the option numbers and potential prices, how do you get Shelly to make the first offer? Are you certain this is the house for you? During your conversation with Shelly at the topo-board, after asking about the options and how long a house has been available, you will say to her, "It would be really nice if I could see a finished house that wasn't a model, to see what your homes really look like. Could I take a look at a couple?" What you want to do is see the inside of the house you're interested in to inspect it without letting Shelly know you're interested in buying it. She may come with you to view these houses, or she may let you go alone. After you're convinced it's the house for you, strike up another conversation with Shelly, stating how you are mildly interested in the house, but point out to her that you can not add any options to the house—even if you hadn't planned to add more. You're setting it up as a "less than perfect" house that you would be settling for if you bought it. Ask Shelly, "Are there any incentives to buy this house?"

Now Shelly should be surprised because you've never once indicated that you could buy so quickly. Most likely, she'll ramble off a percentage amount or dollar figure as a discount for buying the house. This is your starting point because Shelly just spoke a number first. Plus, from your earlier conversation, you know if this house is a spec or previously owned. You're now in the position of strength because you know the amount the builder collected for any options in the house and how much they are ready to start giving away to get it off their hands. All you need to do now is respond to Shelly with a fair offer.

In both of the previous examples, you were able to get big savings because of Insider information. You made an informed offer that in most cases the builder would accept. Be aware, we have had buyers come into our office and "go fishing," offering something ridiculous to see how far we would go down on our price. We do not recommend lowballing a builder with a frivolous offer. We have actually terminated negotiations in such situations if we felt that a buyer was not being sincere. Remember, this is the builder's business; a good, informed offer opens the door for a good deal. If the builder is not willing to meet your price, he will make a counteroffer, which you may counter in return. You will be negotiating for the best price that you can get; you would run the risk of blowing the deal if you made a completely unreasonable offer at first. Insiders don't blow deals; instead, they make good, informed offers and get great savings. So let's move on to the next scenario and discover how to save there.

Negotiating for a Home Under Construction

In this example, we're still at Shelly's community, and we'll use the same house; however, we will give it a 16-week building schedule. Currently, the house is in the eighth week of construction; it's halfway completed. When you are negotiating for a home that is currently under construction, the first thing you want to know, again, is whether the home was already purchased. You should already know what the options policy is for this community, but if you're not certain, you should confirm this information before you show an interest in the home that you want. If you do look at a home that was previously purchased, you'll know what portion of the options have been paid for. For our scenario, remember that Shelly told you that 50% of the option price needs to be paid when ordered. This house has $10,000 of options in it, so the previous owner has paid the $5,000 deposit. If the builder you chose requires any amount of a nonrefundable deposit for options ordered, you will be able to make this policy work for your benefit.

You know the builder wants to get paid twice for the same options. Because this house still has a couple of months before it's finished, he will not be as motivated to sell as if it were standing inventory, so you don't want to appear overly interested, either. You want to let Shelly know that you are considering this house, but you really wanted to add some options that are no longer available because of the construction cutoff dates. You want to stress the negatives of the house, which in this case are limited choices for options. The builder must compensate you for this limitation.

In reality, you may have every option that you want, but you don't want to let Shelly know. You want her to think that you are slightly interested in this house and that she is going to have to make a good offer before you would consider buying it. This is just what you want: You want Shelly to make the first offer. It's fine to ask her if there are any incentives. You might say, "Shelly, since this house is already halfway finished, are there any incentives to buy it? After all, if I did buy this house, I would be limited on my option choices." In our scenario, as an Insider you know that the builder has already been paid $5,000 for this house. The offer that Shelly makes will probably not be for the total amount that she can give away. If Shelly is a very good agent, she will not make any offer at all. Every attempt you make to get her to take the bait and make you an offer might fail if she is a master. Be persistent and stress the negatives of the house. Tell Shelly that you really wanted to add a few more things in the house. Even if she offers you something like 1% toward closing costs or some money to use for future options, at least you will have a start.

You know that your negotiations will start from whatever Shelly offers you to buy the home. You know that $5,000 has already been paid. Let's assume you plan to add $3,000 in options to this home to make it just the way that you want it. So this is what the total price of this home looks like now:

Base price of the home	$200,000
Options already ordered	10,000
Options you ordered	3,000
Total price	$213,000

If you paid $213,000 for this house, the builder would be getting paid an extra $5,000 for options. An Insider would offer $205,000 for the total price of the home to include the options that you want. This would be an extra $8,000 savings for you, and the builder would still be getting close to the full price for this home.

The offer you make	$205,000
Amount of options already paid	5,000
Total price	$210,000

Remember, the builder has already been paid $5,000 from the previous owner, so the builder is only discounting the price of the home by $3,000. This is a reasonable discount for a home already under construction, especially when considering the builder's profit. It is a good deal for the builder and a great deal for the Insider, and that is you.

If you are looking at a home that is already under construction, then the amount of savings you get will directly correspond to the amount of construction that is already finished. The closer the home gets to being finished, the more the builder will be motivated to sell. You will also be in a stronger position to get savings if you know that a previous buyer has already paid for options. Now let's look at the same house under construction, and we will consider it a spec house.

We know the price of the house is $210,000 and you will be adding $3,000 in options, for a total price of $213,000. You have to look closely at the builder's incentive to sell this house. It's under construction, and it will be done in about two months. If he has not had a lot of interest in this house, then he will want to move it fast. Of course, it is difficult for you to know how much interest has been shown on this home because Shelly will tell you she has several people interested. You remember, of course, that Shelly wants to create a sense of urgency in order to sell it; plus, she doesn't want you to think it's a lemon.

There is one way to get an idea of the interest level, and that is to look at the topo-board again. See how many models of the same house are on the board and how many are sold. If the model that you have picked out is very scarce on the board, then maybe it is a tough sell for the builder. If he has several of these models on the board that are marked sold, then it may be because it's selling very well.

One way to get a clear idea is to count how many homes of this model have not sold yet. If the builder has several, he may have trouble selling it, or he may have plotted too many. Some models will yield larger profit margins than others, and builders like to build as many of these as they can. This can lead to plotting more than the market will bear. If you see several unsold homes on the topo-board that is your model, then you can count on the builder being a little more motivated. If an Insider finds out that the builder has overplotted a certain model, he will offer the same amount for a spec house as he would offer for a previously purchased home. In this case, it would be $205,000. Even though the builder will be making a smaller profit, he knows that he has mistakenly plotted more of these homes than the market will bear. If he doesn't get these homes sold within two months, they will become standing inventory and then he will start taking a much bigger loss of profit.

Another motivating factor for the builder is created when he is nearing the end of the community. Builder's love to "close out" communities, and if your home falls in this time frame, you can get big savings. When a builder constructs a community, he will do it in phases. He may have 10 phases before he finishes the whole community. As each new phase opens, the price of the homes will go up. This means that the homes at the end of the community yield a larger profit for the builder. If your home fits into this category, you can offer less for the home and probably still get the deal. For the home we are using as an example, the total cost is $213,000, including the options that you want. The builder will make a total profit of $19,200 dollars on this home; this covers his 7% house profit along with all of the options ordered. The builder is eager to get out of this community; this home is already half finished and no one has bought it yet. An Insider would offer $200,000 for the total price. This would still allow the builder to make a $6,200 profit on the home, and it would get one of his last homes sold to get him out of the community.

Why would a builder take such a big discount? At the end of constructing a community, the builder has probably already started another new community. This means the builder must get construction loans to start on the new project, and he may be limited on the amount he can borrow, until he sells out the previous community. Once all of the homes are sold, the bank will release more funds to the builder to get moving on his next project. If the home you want is holding up these funds, the builder will be very anxious to get rid of it. Cash flow is a concern for all builders but especially smaller ones. We have worked for smaller builders who depended on each sale to get the funds needed to build another house. In one particular community where Jeff worked, the homes sold for an average of $200,000 plus options. At the end of this community, he saw many homes sold at a discount of $15,000 to $20,000 off the complete asking price—awesome deals for the buyers.

Finally, we want to give you one more situation that will motivate a builder. Let's say that during your research you discovered that the builder was a publicly traded company. You also found out what dates his quarters end. If you are looking at a house that is due to close right before a quarter, the builder will be motivated to sell the home. Corporations must report how many closing and sales they have each quarter, and they must show a certain profit. At the end of a quarter, the builder's agents will be pushed to get homes closed, and they will offer incentives to get them sold.

However, the granddaddy of all pushes will come at the end of a corporation's fiscal year. When we have worked for publicly traded builders, we have made some great deals that would make any buyer happy at the end of the fiscal years. You see, at the end of the fiscal year, the builder must make the profits that were promised to the shareholders; these profits only come if the builder meets his closing and selling goals. If the goals are not met, presidents and vice-presidents are fired, and sometimes whole corporate offices are replaced.

If you are looking to buy a house toward the end of the month, then the builder's agent will be trying hard to get you into a contract to meet or exceed her goal. If you are looking at a house near the end of the month and at the end of a quarter, the builder and the agent will be dying to get you into a contract. But, if you are looking to buy a house near the end of the month, at the end of a quarter, and at the end of the fiscal year, you may have hit the jackpot. Timing is everything and can make the difference of thousands of dollars in discounts that you can receive. Your good research you did in chapter 7 will really pay off when you start the negotiation phase.

All of the previous examples are real-world scenarios. The amount that you will be able to save will depend on your detective skills to determine if the house was previously owned or if it was a spec home. If the model you like is overplotted, then you will get to save money. When you negotiate at the end of a quarter or at the end of a fiscal year, you save even more money. If you find a house at a community closeout, you take advantage of the timing to save money. In a perfect world, you will find the house of your dreams that is standing inventory, previously owned with all options paid for, and it is located in a community that is closing out. Just to make it better, the builder overplotted this model, and you're buying it at the end of the builder's fiscal year. Now that you are an Insider, just imagine how much money you could save in this situation.

Negotiating for a Home That Has Not Been Started

You have just read several ways to save big money when you buy a standing inventory home or a home that is under construction. But suppose you don't want to move in right away, or maybe you can't. You might have a home to sell in order for you to buy a new one, or you might be in a firm lease. Don't worry, because Insiders know how to save money in every situation.

Let's say you have found a model that you really like, and the phase is just getting ready to open. In fact, the area of the community that you want is just now being graded into lots. You know several reasons to make a builder deal once the home is under construction, but you're asking why a builder would give discounts on a home that he hasn't even started. Insiders can give several reasons why builders will still make a deal.

First of all, you already know one big reason—timing. Suppose you are buying from a publicly traded builder near the end of the month and at the end of the quarter. Even if the house hasn't been started, the builder still needs to show a certain amount of sales for the month and the quarter. The more he can show, the better he will look. The builder's agent also has sales goals to hit. She will always be more open to making a deal at the end of the month than at the beginning. If your purchase can coincide with the end of a fiscal year, then you will always get a great deal. There is really no way for you to find out if the builder is behind on his goals for the quarter or the fiscal year; the builder's agent knows, but she is not going to tell you. The way for you to know is by trying to read just how eager Shelly is to make a deal. If you find Shelly on the floor, wrapped around your ankle as you are trying to leave the office, then it's a pretty good sign that she and the builder need a few more sales to meet goals. Just kidding, Shelly will not want to get her clothes dirty, but you get the idea.

Because of these sales goals, an Insider knows he can offer less money for the house at the end of the month and even less at the end of the quarter. An Insider will try to go even further if it's at the end of the fiscal year. For example, if we were looking at a $200,000 house at the end of the month that did not fall on a quarter, we would compute what the builder's profit would be and offer a price that would give us 25 percent of the builder's profit. Now let's say we planned on adding $10,000 in options for a total price of $210,000:

Base price of house	$200,000
Options you order	10,000
Total price	$210,000

The builder's profit would be 7% of the base price—$14,000, and 40% of the options—$4,000. This would give him a total profit of $18,000. Our offer would be $205,500, and that gives us a 25% piece of the builder's profit, or a savings of $4,500.

$$\begin{array}{r} \$14,000 \times 25\% = \$3,500 \\ + \ \$4,000 \times 25\% = \$1,000 \\ \hline \text{Your savings} = \$4,500 \end{array}$$

If you write the contract for a deal like this, the builder's agent may write it or describe it as if you are paying the full price for the house and taking the entire discount from the options. That's just fine, as long as you get your discount. Each builder has his own preferred method of reflecting where the discounts are offered.

But the builder is really not motivated to make a deal at this stage of construction, so why would he take this offer? He may not, and chances are that he will counter you with a higher price. An Insider would argue that we are worth the discount because we are already preapproved by a competent lender. This is where your preapproval letter from a well-known local lender will give you clout. We would also state, "Our deal would never fall out be-cause we're going to pay the deposit for our options at the time of contract." A builder will see you as a much more important buyer because he doesn't have to worry about your qualifying for a loan. He will also like the fact that you can pay the required deposit for your options at contract. Because you are paying for your options, he knows he will have a concrete deal. He might just go for it.

You might make this deal anytime, but wouldn't it make more sense to wait until the end of the month or, even better, to make the offer at the end of the quarter? Of course, if it will fit into your schedule, the best time would be at the end of the fiscal year. Having a loan preapproval and being able to pay the deposit for your options at the time of contract will always give you more clout. If you are buying from a builder who doesn't answer to stockholders, then the quarter will not really help you. But every builder has a monthly sales goal that he would like to meet. The end of the month will still be important to him and the best time for you to make your offer.

Insiders also know they can save money on a home that hasn't been started if it's in the last phase of a community. You can get good savings on the last phase because the sooner the builder sells out, the sooner he can borrow more money for the next community. Because you are preapproved for a loan and will be paying the option deposit at the time of contract, he knows you are a "done deal" that won't fall out. With more buyers like you, the builder can get the money from the bank for his next project much earlier. Plus, the sooner a builder can sell out his community, the sooner he can shut down the sales office and close the models.

The sales office is usually located in one of the models. Most builders sell the models right after they're opened and then lease them back from the owners to use for show while the community is selling. Once all the homes are sold, the builder can close the models and stop paying rent. When you buy a house in the last phase, you are taking him one step closer to eliminating very expensive lease payments for the models; this provides motivation for the builder to sell his last houses. The builder will be motivated and offer better deals even if the house hasn't yet been started.

When your looking for that perfect home to bargain for, you want to remember to look at a few things besides the house itself. The location of your lot within the community and direction the house faces should make a big difference on your decision to buy. We covered the differences between lots in chapter 3, but you can use these differences to negotiate a better price. For example, suppose the house you want faces west in a warm sunny climate. You can use this fact as a negative and tell Shelly that you are going to pay higher utility bills because of the sun shining through your windows. Shelly cannot change the direction of the house, but she may be more willing to give a little more toward options because you recognize this negative feature of the home.

The home location that you have picked out might have a lot premium. You will remember that lot premiums are an extra fee that builders charge for a more desirable location or for a larger lot. Lot premiums are pure profit for the builder. If you are buying an oversized lot, you can expect to pay more because you are getting more land. Just how much more is the question.

Suppose you find a standing inventory home with a total price of $215,000. Included in this price is $10,000 for options and $5,000 for a lot premium because it sits on a larger lot than the standard-sized lot. Previous scenarios have shown how much you should offer for the price of the house, and the same basic rules apply to lot premiums with some slight changes. Because the lot premiums are pure profit, an Insider would not offer to pay anything for it on a standing inventory home. It doesn't matter if it was prepurchased or not. The builder may counter with another offer, but on a standing inventory home you should be able to get at least a 50% discount on the premium. If the lot isn't any larger than the standard size, you should try to get the whole premium removed. If the builder is charging more for the house because it is a corner, then you tell him reasons you see this as a disadvantage. For example, you could tell him not only will you have two streets of traffic going by your house, but that children will constantly be running across your front yard for a shortcut to another street. If the builder is highly motivated to sell, he will waive the premium completely.

If you have a premium on a lot where the home is halfway completed, then you will need to pay a little more of the premium, especially if the lot is bigger than the standard size. But you should still try to get the premium waived completely. Start with zero and then come up as the builder counters your offers.

Lot premiums vary widely from builder to builder. This is because there is no way to compute the exact value of a lot from one neighborhood to the next. In many cases, the builder's agent is the one who determines what lot premiums will be. We have set lot premiums in several communities where we have worked; we set the price at what we felt we could get. We've also known agents who set the premiums higher with the expectation that they would discount it when negotiating for the house. To the buyer, it appeared as though they'd been given a concession, when in reality they paid the lot premium the agent wanted to get. That's why premiums are always negotiable. Lot premiums are common when you are next to a golf course or if you have a view. But no matter what the reason is for the premium, just remember that it is pure profit, and it can be negotiated down.

Techniques to Use in All Negotiations

So far, we have talked about getting the best price for your new home; you know that the first one to make an offer is going to lose. But there is more negotiating than just getting the best price. You also want to set some conditions on the sale that will make sure the builder knows he has to build your house with extra care. Now that you have negotiated a great price for your home, you want to reinforce the fact that you are going to be a Crawler.

Before you start going through the contract with Shelly, you need to remind her that you will be videotaping the construction process. Shelly has already agreed to this, but it's still important to remind her at this point. Shelly has probably not mentioned you to her superintendent yet. Now that you are buying a home there, you want to make sure she tells her superintendent that you are a Crawler. After reminding her about videotaping the construction, she'll be certain to inform her super of your intentions and that you'll be watching the construction process from the start to finish. If you buy a partially completed home, you can still videotape the remainder of the building process. If you buy a standing inventory home, you'll videotape the house in its current condition and the finishing touches of construction.

While you are on the subject of reminders, you want to confirm with Shelly the type of construction warranty you will be receiving. All builders will give a one-year builder's warranty. This is your bumper-to-bumper warranty that covers everything in the house. You will also want what is typically called a *2-10 year warranty*. This is usually offered by an insurance company that will cover the plumbing and electrical components of the house for the first two years and give you a ten year warranty on structural defects. But don't be too impressed; this type of warranty is not as good as it sounds. Each one has several exclusions, but it's better to have some additional warranty beyond the builder's one-year coverage plan.

An important question you need to raise about any warranty is who will be responsible for the warranty work. Will it be an outside agency, a subcontractor, the builder, who? If the warranty states that the builder is responsible to do the work, make sure the builder understands this point. We've worked for a builder who included an additional warranty and didn't even realize that they were responsible for the first two years of warranty service.

You also want to confirm your meeting time with the superintendent. Tell Shelly it will not take more than ten minutes of the super's time. You know he is busy, but it is very important for you to meet with him because you want to know the person who will be building your home. You may have met him during your research, but you definitely want to meet with him now. You'll be introducing yourself as a buyer to him and pointing out which house will be yours. Some superintendents will not like meeting the buyers, but because you have researched this superintendent and he has done a good job at his past and current communities, then he should be happy to meet with you. It's very important for you to make that contact, so be firm on this issue. Don't settle for an answer like, "I'm sorry, but it is against company policy." Tell Shelly that you must be able to meet with the super, and it has to be done within one week of the contract date. You see, the sooner you meet him as a new buyer, the better because the construction process typically moves quickly. You want the super to know you as soon as possible so he can start watching your home extra close.

The next item you will demand is a frame-walk of the house. As we discussed earlier, a frame-walk is important to look for any mistakes in the building process. It also gives you another face-to-face with the superintendent. By asking for these two appointments with the super, you are further cementing the thought in Shelly's mind that you are a Crawler. You want to keep stressing this fact to Shelly because it will encourage her to inspect your house while it's being built. She knows that if there are any mistakes, she is going to be the one to hear about it. So she will make a special point of looking over your house at each stage of construction to make sure there are no mistakes. When we had a Crawler buy a house from us, we watched every step in the construction of the house; if we found mistakes, we brought it to the super's attention right away. We didn't want the buyer to see it and come back to us. You want the builder's agent to pay this kind of attention to your house.

As you go through your contract, you must read everything and ask questions about anything that you don't understand. You will be required to leave a check for an earnest money deposit that will be refunded to you if the builder does not accept your offer. In most cases, this will not be an issue because the new-home agent will either know the limits of what she can accept as an offer or has already talked to her boss and received a verbal acceptance of your offer. Writing a complete contract usually takes about two hours, and most agents don't want to waste time on a possible rejection. We wouldn't even take the time to write a contract if we had any doubts about its being accepted. If your offer is much lower than the builder's agent thinks she can get approved, she will most likely contact her boss and make sure that she gets the verbal approval first before going to the writing stage.

When you do write the contract, you need to ask Shelly when you will receive a copy of the contract signed by the builder. At the time you sign your contract, you should receive a copy of everything you signed in the sales office. DO NOT EVER, UNDER ANY CIRCUMSTANCES, LEAVE THE SALES OFFICE WITHOUT A COPY OF EVERYTHING IN YOUR CONTRACT. This contract will not be officially approved, or agreed upon, until the builder or his designee signs it, because your deal is not legally binding until both parties have signed the contract. You need to remember that the builder's agent is only a representative for the builder, and she does not have approving authority. Sometimes it can take two weeks to get a signed copy from the builder. We have even seen it take over a month if the builder is large enough and the corporate office is slow. You should get a signed copy within one week, and we recommend that you keep asking the builder's agent to get it for you if you haven't received one in that time.

The special conditions we've been discussing can and probably should be included in the contract by using addendums. For example, you may be buying a standing inventory house, and you are having the builder add an option or they need to repair something. You can state these conditions along with the time frame to have the actions completed in an addendum. Or, let's say you have negotiated a nonstandard option to be included in your home at no charge; this could be written on an addendum. You might want to purchase a nonstandard item, but only if it costs under a certain amount; your addendum might state that you want to purchase backyard landscaping from the builder, but only if it costs under $2,000. The builder will research the cost, and if he can't sell it to you for $2,000 or less, then it won't be included in the deal. If you have negotiated a deal that includes many options at no cost, then you want to make sure that it is stated so in your contract. If there is no option form to state this fact plainly, then you can have an addendum written to list everything that you are supposed to get.

Addendums are there to clarify and explain all conditions of a contract. Insiders never leave a sales office until everything is written out and explained clearly. You may require ten addendums to be written to cover everything in your deal, but that's fine as long as everything is clear and it is in writing. The key here is "in writing." Legally, you are only protected by what was written down, so make sure you cover all your bases when you've agreed to purchase a house.

There is one addendum that we feel is imperative, and we suggest that you ask for and be very firm about getting it included in your contract. It is the Homebuyer's Protection Addendum (HPA), and Shelly will dread hearing you bring it up again. She may have already told you the builder will not accept this addendum; this is because the builder doesn't want to be forced into completing the home on time. When you researched this builder, we hope you discovered that the homes built were mostly completed at the time of closing. If they weren't completed then, you shouldn't be writing a contract with this builder anyway. The HPA demands that the builder have everything done in your home before you move in.

Shelly may tell you that she cannot make this addendum a part of the contract. If she does say this, ask her why. All you are trying to do is to get the builder to agree to finish the house before you move in. Ask Shelly why the builder cannot make this commitment. Shelly will be really stuck to find a good answer because there aren't any. Ask her to include the addendum even if she doesn't want to do so. Tell her if her boss rejects the contract, then you would like her boss to explain why the builder cannot promise to finish the house before you move in. If, after all your attempts, they still wont' accept the HPA as a part of your contract, don't despair. If you go forward with the purchase, remember you still have your Crawler reputation and the videotaped construction to protect you when it comes time to close. Plus, in chapter 11, we'll be giving you a few pointers about the closing process.

At this point, if Shelly had any doubts about you being a Crawler, they are gone. Shelly knows now that you don't just talk a good game, but you are ready to back everything up in writing. Because the HPA is a new concept in the building industry, we expect it to be initially received with resistance from builders; but given your efforts and a little time, we're confident it will become a common addendum in the industry.

Right now, even the good builders don't want to be legally bound to have their homes completed before the homebuyers move in. They want the freedom to force you to close on your home and then come back after you have taken possession to fix their mistakes. The bad builders, on the other hand, want this same freedom, but the difference is they never intend to come back and fix their mistakes. The builder's contracts are written to force you to move into your home even though it is not complete. In other words, you must pay the builder completely for your home before the builder completely finishes it. The HPA will change the rules; it forces the builder to finish your house before he gets full payment. It is the only way to be sure that your home will be complete at the time that you move in. Without the HPA, you will be vulnerable to the Closing Trap, which we will explain in detail in chapter 11.

The Offer and Counteroffer

When you make an offer to a good builder's agent, she knows what she will be able to accept and what she won't. If you offer something that she knows will not be accepted, she will have to make a counteroffer right on the spot. You may have asked for $5,000 off the lot premium price; Shelly may know the maximum discount she can give is $3,000. If she is master, she won't counter with the whole $3,000 discount. Instead, she will offer a $1,000 discount; this way she still has room to negotiate if necessary. A good builder's agent will never give away everything at the beginning of negotiations. She will give only one piece at a time.

A good analogy can be seen with children and a bag of M&Ms. Suppose you want to reward your child every time he does something good. If you have a one-pound bag of M&Ms, are you going to give him the whole bag the first time he does a good deed? If you do, you won't have anything to give him for the next good deed he does. With no rewards, he may stop doing good deeds.

The negotiation works the same way. If Shelly has given away everything right up front and you are not sold, then she has no more incentives to use and she will lose the deal—she'll be out of M&Ms. Shelly will try to give you just one piece at a time until she can get you into a contract, hoping it will only take a few M&Ms to sell you. It's your job to keep taking every piece until the bag is empty. This is done through making offers and counteroffers. As an Insider you have the advantage because you know the approximate profit that the builder is making on his homes. To put it plainly, you know just how many M&Ms Shelly has to give away, so you will negotiate until you get the whole bag. That is the benefit of being an Insider.

The scenarios we have used in this chapter are real world, but the savings that our readers get in different parts of the country will vary according to the circumstances. If you are in a city where there are only five builders and all of them are selling out faster than they can build the houses, you may not be able to get as large of a discount as seen in this book. But if you are in a fast-growing city with a lot of competition for new homes, you may get even larger discounts than the examples we've used. The profit percentages will be about the same for the builders across the country, but if a builder is selling his houses much faster than he can build them, he doesn't really have to give out any discounts at all. You might see this in some communities where there are never any standing inventory homes. If you decide to buy a home in a fast-selling community like this, you may get very little in the way of incentives. You should still get something because you are preapproved and a firm buyer; you know what the profits are for the builder and you should always use this knowledge to ask for discounts. The worse thing that can happen is the builder will say no. The best thing that can happen is you'll get what you want; but that will never happen if you don't ask.

The Contract

The new-home contract will vary to some degree in different states across the country. It will also be different from builder to builder. However, there are two facts about every contract that do not change, regardless of the location or the builder. The first fact is that a lawyer wrote the contract; the second is that it was written for the sole benefit of the builder. A contract will contain the main purchase agreement, and it may have several attachments. These attachments may be called *exhibits* or *addendums*. They will be used to describe special circumstances that pertain to the community where you are buying a home. They might describe the fact that you are near an airport, or they might tell you what the homeowner's association dues are. All of these attachments arc considered a legal part of the contract to purchase your home and you must read them very carefully. Hopefully, one of these attachments will be the Homebuyer's Protection Addendum.

Although it's impossible to name every aspect of every contract in this book, there are several things that we want you to know. In the beginning of the contract, it will describe how and where your earnest money deposit will be kept. Usually, it directs the buyer to write the deposit check out to a neutral third party like a title company, which will create a separate earnest money account. Some contracts want the check written directly to the builder. We have worked for some builders who require the earnest money to be deposited in their own account. In the states that do allow the builder to deposit earnest money into their own account, they will usually require it to be a separate account. This means the builder must have an operating account and another account just for earnest money deposits. The builder should not be able to touch the earnest money until it is time to close on escrow.

This sounds fair enough on the surface, but it doesn't always work out that way. We have seen builders access these accounts and take money before the closing of escrow. As long as the house closes without problems, there's not much reason for concern. But what if the builder is having financial difficulty? What if, for some reason, you wanted out of the deal? It's a lot harder to get your money back when the builder has it in his own account, or he has spent it. But there is another very important reason to not want your money in your builder's account. Suppose your builder goes bankrupt? Do you think you will have a chance of getting your money back? If it was kept in an escrow account, it would be protected, but if it's in the builder's account, you'll lose it. The research that you did in chapter 7 will help you determine how financially sound your builder is, but things can change in this industry very quickly. Insiders know that their money is much safer in an escrow account, and that is where they will demand the deposit to be placed.

The next item we want to cover is the expected completion date of your home. If you are buying a home that has not been started, the builder will give you an estimation of the completion date. If the builder has a 16-week building schedule, then Shelly will tell you to expect delivery of the house in about four or five months. Shelly will also be able to give you a more accurate date once building is underway. You should always get at least a 30-day notice of when the closing date will be. Now all of this sounds fair and reasonable, but what does the contract actually say? You will have a section in your contract that will state something like the following:

> Because of the nature of the homebuilding industry, it is difficult to estimate the exact delivery date of a new home. Due to a variety of factors, the estimated closing date can be extended for weeks or even months. Buyer and seller agree that the completion of the home will take place within 12 months of the date of this contract.

Even though the builder's agent has told you that your house will be ready in four or five months, you are actually agreeing that it could take a year. If your builder decides to delay construction of your home for any reason, you are legally bound to wait up to a year from the day you signed the contract before you can cancel the sale. We have seen countless new-home communities delayed by builders for several reasons. Every year thousands of new homeowners' lives are thrown into turmoil because their homes have been delivered several months after the original estimation date. The contract that you sign will not protect you from these delays, and every new-home contract has this section in it. Some contracts we've seen have even given the builder up to 18 months to complete a house. The only way to avoid this agony is to do the research outlined in chapter 7.

The next section of the contract that we want to discuss are the obligations for a builder to deliver a completed home. Now you as a new-home buyer probably think that a completed new home is fully constructed with everything clean and in perfect working order. Common sense tells you if your home is brand new then everything should be perfect and finished, right? Well, let us tell you what the builder considers a completed home. He considers a completed home one that can be issued a Certificate of Occupancy. It doesn't matter if the home is finished or not. It only matters if the home can be legally occupied. There could be 100 or more defects or unfinished items, but it can still be legally occupied. This is all that the builder is required to do to fully perform all of his obligations as outlined in your contract.

When you were talking to Shelly, did she mention this little fact to you? No, she did not; she was busy trying to make you feel good about your Harley or some other subject. She was telling you about the quality that goes into her homes. The last thing that Shelly wants to point out to you is that the contract is written to catch you in the Closing Trap. Chapter 11 is dedicated to explaining the Closing Trap, but can you see again how important your research is going to be? You want to be sure that your builder and the superintendent are completing their houses on time with fewer than ten items on the punch list from the walk-through.

You now know that the builder does not have to finish the home before he can force you to close an escrow. So what if you just refuse to close if the house looks terrible and there are 50 or 60 defects in the house? There is another section in the contract that will read something like this:

> If buyer does not fully perform when obligated to do so, then seller may grant an extension to buyer. Buyer will pay $100.00 a day for said extension and will be due and payable at the closing of escrow.

Shelly will not want to spend a lot of time on this section of the contract either. She will not want to reveal how the Closing Trap works. In the previous excerpt, you would be required to pay $100.00 a day if you tried to delay the closing date. You would end up paying a lot of money to extend the closing of the home; the builder has nothing limiting him from delaying a closing.

Let's recap what we have learned about the contract so far. First of all, they are written by lawyers for the builder's benefit. Next, the builder has up to one year, sometimes longer, to finish your home. The builder doesn't even have to finish the home in order to force you to close. He only needs to get a Certificate of Occupancy, whether the house is finished or not. You as the buyer, on the other hand, must close on your home within five days after the Certificate of Occupancy is issued, whether the house is finished or not. If you don't then you can be charged $100.00 a day or more as a penalty.

Such a deal! Where do I sign? Unfortunately, all the new-home contracts from all of the larger builders are written this way. They are written with the intention of catching you in the Closing Trap. But don't worry, because we know how to stay out of the Closing Trap, and after you finish this book, you will not become a victim either. Even though the contract is written against you, your research will rule out any builder who has had problems finishing houses in the past. Also, if you are successful in getting the Homebuyer's Protection Addendum included in your contract, you will not have any problems getting your home completed before you close on escrow.

The facts that we have pointed out about contracts may scare you a little bit. That is okay because we want you to be aware of the disadvantages the average home buyer is up against when he buys a new home. But you are no average home buyer; you are becoming an Insider. Your research will protect you from shoddy new-home builders, and your Crawler status will keep reputable builders under control. But even if your research was lacking and you were not as good a Crawler as you would have liked, we still have more techniques for you to use in chapter 11 to avoid the Closing Trap. We are going to give you every Insider tool to use. The more tools that you use, the better off you will be.

Closing the Deal

After you have made an awesome deal on your new home and signed the contract, you need to confirm a few things. First and foremost is that you need a copy of everything that pertains to the contract and the community. In your previous research, you should have studied the CC&Rs and the HOA rules and regulations to make sure that there is nothing in them that you cannot live with. When you sign a contract, you should get your own copy of each of these documents if you haven't received your own copy already.

You want to confirm the date of your meeting with the superintendent with the builder's agent. If she cannot reach the super at the time of contract, then you will want her to call you the following day to set up the appointment. Don't let this meeting be postponed. Make sure that the agent knows that this could be a deal breaker. If the builder's agent seems to take it lightly or you have doubts about her setting up the meeting, then make it a statement in an addendum to the contract. This will ensure that the builder's agent gets it done.

If there are any unsettled issues, such as the acceptance of the HPA, ask the builder's agent when she will know the answers and when you should expect the call. It's always good to get the builder's agent to commit to a date if she is doing something for you. Setting a date will motivate her to get it done. Look at your checklist. Are there any questions that were left unanswered? Have you thought of any new questions you need answered? Are you unsure about anything at this point? If you are, make sure you get the answers that you need and the clarification about anything that seems unclear before you leave the office.

Chapter Summary

Are you excited yet? We are, just talking about making great deals. We wish we could be there with you when you negotiate your awesome new-home deal. We hope you remember to write us and tell us all about it.

Anyway, let's recap what we have covered in this chapter. When you negotiate the purchase price of your new home, you must remember that the first one to name a price will lose. Always get the builder's agent to offer an incentive or some savings before you make any offers. You will consider anything that the builder's agent offers as freebies, and you'll start your negotiating from that point.

We explained the profit margins so that you can compute a reasonable offer and still get great savings. Isn't it wonderful to know what the builder can afford to give away? With the information you have learned so far in this book, you are becoming an Insider. Hopefully, you'll have several new-home communities in your area to choose from that meet your standards, and you will be able to use the profit margins to save thousands of dollars.

Insiders know that all prices must be in writing before a contract is written. You never want to sign a contract for a new home unless you know all of your option prices. There may be slight exceptions for options that are under $100, such as an extra wall outlet that you decided on or a nicer ceiling fan. You aren't going to get hit with a major cost for these minor items. It is still best to include everything that you can when you sign the contract because you can always get a better deal for the house if you buy the options at the time of signing. Having everything in writing will protect you and ensure that you get what you negotiated.

Timing is an important factor that you can use to get a better price on a new home. If you can buy right before a quarter ends, you will find a more accommodating builder's agent. If you can buy at the end of a fiscal year or at the end of a community, you can save even more. Of course if these factors coincide with a standing inventory home that has had the options already paid for, you might just hit the jackpot.

In our brief section on contracts, we wanted to show how much the contract is written against you. We were trying to demonstrate how important it is for you to follow our guidelines. Doing good research and being a great Crawler may be the best tools that you have to ensure quality in your new home. We don't want any of our readers to ever become a victim of the Closing Trap.

We've given you several real-world scenarios and techniques to use to negotiate a great deal. Your success will depend on using everything in this book as your guide, your prowess as a negotiator, and the market where you're buying your new home. You might negotiate much better deals than we have given here, and you might not get as good as a deal as in our examples. If you live in a city that has very little building and the builders are selling homes faster than they can build them, your discounts will be limited. Then again, you might dazzle a builder and walk away with a terrific deal. Demand will affect the purchase price in new homes just as it would in any other product. But isn't it great to know that in any market you will have the skills to get the best deal possible?

Chapter 9

The Building Process: Become a Crawler

In this chapter:

- The Superintendent
- The Power of the Video Camera
- The Construction Schedule
- Being a Crawler with Tact
- The Frame-Walk
- Chapter Summary

Builders have a dream of the perfect new-home buyer. It's a person who comes into their community, buys a house on the very first visit, and asks no questions. This perfect buyer never comes to the construction site while the house is being built and is never heard from until the house is done. This buyer will not complain about any defects found on the walk-through because he trusts the builder to return and fix them. Sound like anyone you know? You may not believe it, but sadly a lot of the new-home buyers today could almost fit into this dream description.

You, on the other hand, are not the dream client. For the builder, Insiders fall more into the nightmare category than into the dream category. We don't mean to say that you are going to be ugly, unprofessional, or rude. You are simply going to demand that your house be built right the first time. You have this wild belief that if you are going to pay 100% for your home at the time it closes, then you expect it to be 100% done. To be even more unreasonable, you are going to demand that it is built correctly. As Insiders we do not believe it is unreasonable to expect a quality built complete home at the time of closing. Unfortunately most builders do consider this unreasonable, but here is the most important point: Every builder who is constructing new homes today can build a complete quality home when properly motivated.

You've already been branded as a Crawler, and now it is time to live up to that reputation. We want Shelly and the superintendent to see a big "C" on your forehead every time you come into their community. Plus, for your benefit the super and the builder's agent should become a part of your extended family; you want them to know you well and respect you even more. So let's walk through the building process together and get to know our new family. If you are using a Realtor, she can do everything in this chapter.

The Superintendent

The first step that Insiders take during the building process is to meet with the superintendent. This is the meeting you arranged with Shelly when closing the deal on your house. During your various meetings with Shelly, you established yourself as a very smart buyer who definitely is going to be a Crawler. Shelly should have already briefed the super about you, and now it is time to meet him face-to-face. To make this exchange of information easier, we're going to give your super a name; for the rest of this book, "Ron" will be your superintendent.

Before your first meeting with Ron, you will have already completed the research on his building record, not only in this community but in the one he worked at before this one. If you've been extra ambitious, you have researched even more of his communities. You can never do too much research, and the more you do, the better. When you meet with Ron, you want to compliment him on his earlier work. In fact, you could tell him that he was a large part of your decision to buy in this community, which may be very true. Everyone loves a compliment, and Ron gets very few from home buyers. He'll really appreciate your taking the time to tell him how good he is. He will also realize in the back of his mind that you are every bit the Crawler that Shelly said you were.

After starting off by complimenting Ron and making him feel good, you want to reinforce your Crawler status. You might say to

Ron, "I will be videotaping the construction because I want to be able to look back at my dream home on film and watch it as it was built." This is more than reasonable, and Ron should realize this immediately. In many communities where we've worked, we would go out and take pictures for our buyers so they could see their homes at different stages of construction. These pictures were just for memory, but your videotaping will have a more important purpose.

You should go on to say to Ron, "I think having a videotape of the construction would be great proof of the quality that went into my home. Don't you agree?" Ron will most likely say yes because there isn't much else he can say. You might even ask Ron, "Do you prefer that I come after hours to film, or is it okay to film during the day as long as I stay out of the way of all of the subcontractors?" You want Ron to know that you are not just talking about it, but that you are definitely going to film his work. You might also say, "I understand that sometimes mistakes are made by the subcontractors. And if something is found on the film, should I bring it to your attention directly or just tell Shelly?" He will probably say that if you have any concerns you should go to Shelly because he does not have the time to talk to home buyers every day and he is right. You already know this anyway, but again it is important for you to reinforce your Crawler status with him.

So far in your initial meeting with Ron, you have made some very important points. You have told him how good you think he is and let him know that you have researched his past performance. You have also let him know that you will be watching closely with the video camera. If you have the time to talk a little bit more, you might try to find something in common with him that will make him feel good about you. Remember the scenario with the Harley that Shelly tried to use on you? You can use the same technique on Ron and, if successful, you will have just made a friend. It's important for you to establish rapport with Ron, but it is also important to establish respect. At this point, you have done both and it might be time to end the meeting. A good ending would be something like, "Ron, I know you are very busy and I really appreciate your taking the time to talk with me. I can now see why so many other homeowners were so happy with your work. I look forward to talking with you again. I'll see you at the frame-walk if I don't see you before then."

The meeting might take only ten minutes of your time. We want to point out that if you are using a Realtor, then both of you should be at this meeting. The Realtor can do all of the video-taping if you prefer, but you must be at the initial meeting with Ron. You see, you want Ron to warm up to you more than your Realtor because it's your house he's building. If Ron likes the Realtor, it isn't going to make much of a difference on your house because he still doesn't know the people moving into it. So make sure you are there.

The Power of the Video Camera

If you have purchased a standing inventory home, then obviously you will not be videotaping the complete construction process. But you should still go in and videotape the inside of the house, especially if you see any cracks in the concrete slab. You will want to take a close-up of any cracks and see if you can insert a nickel into the crack. If you can, there might be a problem with the foundation. A basic rule of thumb is that foundation slab cracks should not be any wider than a nickel; if you can slide one into a crack, you must have it repaired. The videotape will prove the crack exists, and you will want to visually see the repair work they've done before your flooring is installed over it. Don't take the builder's word that the repairs were made; we've seen homes where several cracks were quickly covered up by the flooring with no repair work done, and the buyer was told the repairs had been made.

You should also videotape the cabinets, countertops, walls, and any tiling to make sure they are all in good condition. When you take the time to videotape the entire house, it forces you to take a very close look at everything. This will help you make sure everything is fixed or finished before you move in.

If you are buying a house where the construction hasn't started yet, you should start the videotaping of the lot before the foundation is poured. This first step in taping will be more for your memories than anything else, but it will give you a complete record of the whole building process. In your first film, we would recommend filming your lot and both of your neighbors. This helps put your house location in perspective.

After the foundation has been poured, you want to film the surface and look for any cracks or breaks around the edges. You also want to pay attention to the drainpipes that are coming up through the slab. Where are they located in the foundation? You want to make certain they are coming up in the proper rooms. We've seen homes where the plumber was working off the wrong plans, and the super didn't catch the misplaced bathroom pipes until it was pointed out to him. The pipes were coming up in what was the hall, not the bathroom—and this super had a good reputation, too. In addition to where your pipes are, you want to make sure they are covered. You don't want anything to be thrown down your drains, especially dirt or chunks of wood or concrete. Any debris that gets caught in the pipes will cause you plumbing problems; those problems might not show up for a couple weeks. So be sure that the drainpipes are always covered; if they are not, ask Shelly to go to Ron and get them covered. Make sure that you get any uncovered drains on the videotape.

When the framing stage of construction starts, you will want to pay close attention to the wood being used. Is it full of cracks? Look and film close-ups of the joints between the wood studs and see how well they are nailed together. There should not be any gaps between two pieces of wood nailed together. We have seen several cases where a horizontal 2 × 4 will be put in place between the vertical studs to support a showerhead. This small piece of wood sometimes will have a 2-inch gap between its end and the vertical frame structure, and the nails are clearly visible. This support brace stays in place during the construction period, but it won't last long after the homeowner moves in and starts adjusting their showerhead back and forth. It will soon become loose, and the only way to fix it is to tear out the shower wall.

Another common area for gaps is between ceiling beams, where a light fixture or ceiling fan will be attached. Heavy fixtures will cause this weak brace to falter quickly. When it goes, it's a hole in your ceiling you have to repair, not to mention the electrical wires affected. If you pick up gaps or really bad wood on your videotape, you should bring it to Shelly's attention immediately to get it fixed. When you find something that needs to be fixed, you must always check to make sure that it's done. If you were the only one who noticed the problem, then the chances are good that you are the only one who will make sure that it is corrected.

After the framing stage, you will start to see the plumbing and electrical work being done. When you are filming this stage, you might notice that the bathtubs are installed. The bathtubs must always be covered up with something more than plastic.

The subcontractors are not as careful as you would like, and it's very easy for one to drop a hammer or something on the tub, causing chips and even cracks. If the tub is not covered with a solid material, these damages are inevitable, and you end up seeing them on your walk-through. You also don't want subcontractors throwing sawdust and other garbage down your drains. You know from your research that Ron will keep a clean working environment, but you don't want that cleanliness to be a result of the subcontractors dumping things down your drains.

After all of the electrical and plumbing items are in the house, you will be scheduled for your frame-walk. This is another appointment that you must attend, even if you are using a Realtor. You never want Ron to forget who you are. Your Realtor should be there as well, and she would be the perfect person to do the videotaping. You will want to get Ron in the videotape, so if there are any mistakes found there will be no misunderstandings as to whether Ron knew about them. Ron will be more committed to fix any mistake if he knows there is a record of him seeing it on tape.

The next phase of the construction will be insulation and the outside construction of your home. The outside of your home might be stucco, which is popular in the Southwest, or it might be brick or wood in another part of the country. Whatever the material is, you should get it all on tape. You will have a certain "R factor" in the insulation that is being installed; you should read the description of the insulation to make certain its what you expected. Suppose you have purchased R-15 value insulation and you see them putting in R-13. You would need to bring this to the attention of Shelly right away. It's not important for you to understand every part of a house, but it is important for you to get it on tape. This way, if you ever have a problem in the future, you will have proof that it was a builder's mistake.

After the outer shell of your home is complete, you'll see the drywall going up on the inside. When you film this stage, look for any leaks in the plumbing. If there are any water leaks, they will show up very easily as stains on the drywall. If the drywall absorbed too much water, you want it replaced and not just painted over. You also want to pay attention to how smooth the walls look. Are the seams obvious? Can you see any bowed sections? Clues of this can be seen along the floorboard and if you look across the wall, down the length of the room. If you do see any of these problems, you want to get them repaired or replaced.

The drywall stage is when you really start to see your house taking shape. Once the drywall has been put up, things start to move pretty fast, and this is when most people start to get really excited because they know they will be moving in soon. It doesn't take long for the cabinets, sinks, and light fixtures to go in. Still, you want to film everything once it has been installed. A lot of mistakes can happen at the end of the construction schedule by using the wrong fixtures, such as the wrong faucets. If you have special options that can be seen at this point, you want to make sure you get them on film.

Your last videotape will be taken at the walk-through inspection of your home, sometimes called the *orientation*. Some builders want to breeze you through the house and just orient you to the appliances and electric box. But you, as an Insider, want to inspect the entire house. Because you have closely monitored your home from start to finish, there should not be any defects or punch list items that need to be recorded, but there is always the chance that you and Ron missed something. Not only that, this walk-through may be your first chance to inspect your floor covering if you had the builder install it. So be thorough when inspecting this time, just as you have been every other time. We are going to cover how you should proceed with the walk-through in the next chapter, but you will want to videotape the meeting and get everyone on tape that is there.

When you videotape the construction of your house, you are creating a permanent record of the whole process. You might not have realized something that comes up a couple of years later, and if you go back to the tape, you might be able to prove it was the fault of the builder. If you have filmed a dirty construction area and your drains were exposed, you will have the video as proof, if you ever have plumbing problems, that it was the builder who was negligent. We have seen several plumbers snake drains soon after homeowners move in and come up with pieces of drywall, wood chips, nails, and even fast-food bags. It's hard to get the builder to pay for this expense unless you can prove it was his fault. Your videotape can provide the proof. If you ever need to file any complaints with the state contractor's board, you will have proof that your claim is valid.

Because you have a permanent film record of your home, there is no way a superintendent could cover up any mistakes because you have them on tape. During your new-home search, you made it clear that you are an astute buyer, and you are going to be a Crawler. You have reinforced that reputation after the first meeting with Ron. Now, by videotaping the construction of your house, you have convinced everyone of your Crawler status. It might not even matter if you have film in the camera as far as the super is concerned. You just want him to see you filming so he knows that you are sincere in everything that you do. Of course, we are not suggesting that you leave out the film. We are only trying to make the point that it is just having you there with the camera that will encourage Ron to be at his best.

The Construction Schedule

In chapter 6, we asked you to get a construction schedule from the sales office. Shelly was probably not able to give you one, but you can still get a verbal schedule from her. You want to know how long the house will take to be completed and what is the total building time. All builders will have a time schedule to follow for each phase of the house. If Shelly tells you that it takes about 14 weeks to complete a home, then you should see yours done in about that time. We say "about" because we have seen builders fall behind so many times that you really aren't going to be sure how long it takes until construction has started. If the house you are buying has already been started, you want to ask Shelly what week of construction it is in and when it will be completed. Home buyers who do not research builders have suffered frustration beyond belief. We have seen homes delayed for six to nine months; we've also seen homes that never even got started. We have sold semi-custom homes in one community in the $500,000 range that never got started, and the builder ended up selling out to a different company that came in and finally built the homes. The very patient buyers in this community waited a year and a half to finally see their homes complete.

Aren't you glad that you are an Insider? You have done your research, and you know that your builder will complete his homes on schedule. As you go through the building process, you should see people working every week on your house. If you can't get out to the construction site during the week, make sure your Realtor does if you have one. Even if you can't make it out during the day, you can still go to the construction site after work or on the weekends. The construction crews will be gone, but you should still see the changes made to your house; it's also a nice quiet time to videotape.

You should check in from time to time with Shelly and ask her if your house is on schedule. Sometimes there are legitimate reasons for construction delays. There might be a delay because of a shortage in building supplies or because of the weather. Even in a city such as Las Vegas, where it hardly ever rains, the weather can cause delays. If you live in a part of the country that has severe weather you could be delayed for weeks; usually builders try to anticipate this potential delay during the problem seasons. But, Shelly should always know if there are any delays, and you want her to tell you as soon as she knows anything.

There are some delays that you don't ever want to see. If you ever see a week go by with no work on your house being done, then you want to find out why. If a builder is having financial difficulty, he can fall behind on paying his subcontractors. If he falls too far behind, the subs will stop working until they get paid. Again, your research will prove invaluable because you know that your builder is financially stable, but things can change in a hurry in the building industry. You don't ever want to take anything for granted, not until your house is finished and you are living there happily ever after. So be sure to question what seems like a lull in the work schedule. Shelly will probably have a very good reason for the delay and be happy to explain it to you. And, by asking about it, you are never letting Shelly forget that you are always watching. Both Shelly and Ron will be glad once your home is done and you're out of their hair. But, before that happens, they will want to make sure that if only one home in the community is completed on time, then that one home will be yours.

We have sat in construction meetings when the supers have asked us who is going to be the most difficult to close. The reason they ask is because they are not intending to have the homes completed at closing time, and they want to have the most complete homes go to the most difficult buyers. Crawlers are always at the top of the list. You will be a priority for them, and Ron is going to do everything he can to get your home done perfectly.

Timing is so important, not just for closing on your new home, but in scheduling the move into your new home. You need to arrange moving trucks and maybe a simultaneous closing if you have a house you're selling before you can close on your new one. If you run into delays in the construction, you may need to arrange for storage of your belongings and/or make living arrangements. We suggest giving yourself a cushion of time between when you expect to move into your new home and when you leave your old one. This way you should be less stressed during the move, and if you run into a delay, you've got that cushion in place. If your delay requires more time, you'll have a head start on making alternate plans; but keep this knowledge of a flexible moving time to yourself. This cushion is for your benefit; do not let Shelly know about it, or else you'll lose any sense of priority with her to make certain your home is finished on time. This cushion is to provide you with a less stressful move, not to provide the builder with an excuse for not finishing your home on time.

Being a Crawler with Tact

You need to remember that being a Crawler is not just watching everything, but it's building rapport with Shelly and Ron as well. We know you understand how to keep a watchful eye out during the construction of your home, but there is more to being a Crawler. Anyone can be a complainer, and no one likes people who complain about everything. Your goal as a Crawler is not to make Shelly and Ron mad at you. Your goal is to make them respect and, hopefully, even like you. A good builder's agent will want your house to be perfect when it is done. Shelly really doesn't want to hear anyone complain about anything wrong with their home. Her life would be so easy if every home she sold was finished on time without mistakes. In your case, you want Shelly to go the extra mile; you want her to take a little extra care with your home. A good Crawler not only commands respect but is able to make friends with Shelly and Ron as well.

Shelly knows you are a Crawler and that fact alone will cause her to pay close attention to your home. But, she will go even further on your behalf if she likes you. That is why we have said you will never be rude but professional in asking your probing questions. We want you to be courteous in all of your dealings with Shelly and Ron. A thank-you card to Shelly, or better yet to her boss, will go a long way to winning Shelly's admiration. Vice-presidents love to get "rave letters" about their employees.

If you are developing a good relationship with Ron and Shelly, a good time to write a rave letter is after the frame-walk. You could write one about each of them. Ron doesn't get many rave letters from the home buyers, and he will be especially happy about receiving one from you. You see, both Ron and Shelly know you expect quality work, and writing these letters will show your appreciation when you receive it. This is a great way to develop admiration and respect, or in other words it's how to build rapport. And, you remember what rapport really means!

There are many ways to build your relationships besides sending thank-you cards and rave letters. You could bring a small gift when you stop by the office. It doesn't have to be much; in fact, a favorite is food. Many times, builder's agents can't get away from the office to get lunch, and food is almost always welcome. It could be as simple as a soft drink, donuts, or a pizza. But take the time to find out what Shelly and Ron might like. When you actually bring something in to them, it will show your appreciation for what they are doing for you. These little gestures will go a long way to building rapport, and it can make a major difference in the quality of your home. Shelly and Ron will always think of you as a Crawler, but you want them to think of you as a nice Crawler. To the builder, you will always be just another closing. But to Ron and Shelly, you are going to be a Crawler with a big heart. They will have the most influence over how well your home will be done. First and foremost is to become a Crawler in their mind and earn their respect, but when you build rapport with them, it will almost seem like they are on your side. If they like you and respect you, they will go to bat for you if necessary. Ron will look a little closer at your home if he respects and likes you. Remember, this is an important goal because you want that special attention during the construction process.

The Frame-Walk

We want to say a few more things about the frame-walk. It will be a good measure of the quality that is going into your home. It's at this meeting that you will be going through your complete home and seeing it from the inside out with Ron. You are looking to ensure all the structural options you chose are constructed, plus you're checking for the electric and plumbing options you picked. You should have a diagram with you when you walk the home that shows all of your options that you selected. This way you can go through each room and compare that room with your diagram. It's easy to catch mistakes this way, and they are easily corrected at the framing stage.

The advantage on this frame-walk is having Ron with you to answer any questions you might have, but also to address any mistakes you might come across. Of course you shouldn't expect to see any mistakes at this point. One reason is because you have been filming the house and may have picked them up and had them corrected already. The other reason is because of your Crawler status; both Ron and Shelly have been paying close attention to this home. It's likely that they both have been walking and checking on this house every week to see that it has been built correctly. With their close attention and your videotaping, you could have a perfect frame-walk, and that's what you want.

Another feature you want to look for during the frame-walk is the quality of the wood in the house. Is the wood split? Are the joints meeting flush? You don't want to see big gaps between the framing studs and support braces. Remember all the potential locations we discussed in the previous section. Just be observant as you walk through the rooms. You can also look at the foundation. If it is concrete, are there any cracks? If there is wood sub-flooring, like in a two-story house, is it well secured? Don't hesitate to ask any questions that you may have at this point. It is not often that you will get Ron's full attention. But don't forget to compliment him if the frame-walk goes well. It is always good to keep building rapport.

If you do find any mistakes on the frame-walk, make sure that they are listed in writing. You will have the big extra benefit of filming the mistakes and having them on tape, but you still want everything in writing. Remember, written documentation is extremely important in protecting you and your rights if you ever need to file a complaint with the state. Find out when the corrections will be made so that you can return to film the corrected work. You can tell Ron in a nice way that you plan to do this, again referring to your film record. If you run into a little resistance, tell Ron you will want to be able to show a future buyer that everything in the house was built correctly. He cannot object to this, and it makes him commit to a date. Ron will make sure that it gets done if he knows you are going to be back to film it on a certain date.

After everything has been corrected and your house is moving along perfectly, it is time for you to write your rave letters. These letters will smooth over any confrontations that might have come up at the frame-walk. You will always be firm when dealing with Ron or Shelly, but you will also want to keep up your rapport with them. Rewarding someone with a written compliment when a job is done well is a great way to keep building rapport.

Chapter Summary

The construction process is a very exciting time for Insiders. You are watching your house being created right before your eyes. Because you have done your research and followed the Insider's steps, you should have very few problems at this point. That doesn't mean you will let down your guard. You will only do that after you have moved in and everything in your house is in perfect working order.

You have learned in this chapter how to meet and develop rapport with the superintendent. The first meeting with Ron will confirm you as the Crawler that Shelly said you were. But, it will also start you on a course of building rapport with him. You want to make sure that you compliment Ron on his previous work. He will love the compliment but also understand how thorough you are to even know about his past work.

You should expect the construction process to move on schedule, but you want to have Shelly explain any delays. If you are in a lease or if you are selling your home, you want to give yourself a cushion of time between moving from your old home to the new one. If there are any delays, you will have time if you need to make other arrangements. You know the more flexible that you can be concerning time, the easier it will be for you. But you also know you won't necessarily be sharing the knowledge of this flexibility with Shelly or Ron.

You will get a great opportunity to see quality in your home at the frame-walk. This provides another face-to-face with Ron and allows you to get questions answered. It also gives you the chance to keep building rapport with him. If your frame-walk goes well, then you know that you are doing everything right. If your frame-walk finds several mistakes, then you need to beef up your Crawler status with both Shelly and Ron.

As you can see by now, each chapter is building on the previous one. If you follow all of the guidelines in each step, your building process will be fun and exciting as your home nears completion. If you have neglected to do your research or made a poor impression as a Crawler, you might experience some frustration. We hope that you use every step because we don't want to see you experience any frustration. Insiders avoid frustration by using the steps in this book. And we can't wait to hear about your happy home-buying experience.

Chapter 10

The Walk-Through: Orientation or Inspection?

In this chapter:

- Setting the Walk-Through and Closing Date
- The Builder's Checklist
- The Punch List
- Reschedule if You Have To
- New-Home Nightmares
- Chapter Summary

If you have followed all of the steps in this book so far (*and we know you have*), then your walk-through will be easy. But, if you have a friend who has not read our book, he may have a battle on his hands at this point. So for the sake of your friend, a non-Insider, we want to cover what can happen and what should happen during the walk-through. If your friend is in trouble, then you might suggest he read this book.

We've been a part of hundreds of walk-through appointments, and one fact stands out: Builders do not want home buyers to think of their walk-through as an inspection but as only an orientation. In other words, they do not want you to look over the house with a fine-tooth comb. They simply want you to pay attention to where the circuit breakers are and how to use the appliances and different features in the home.

In your case, once again the builder is not going to get what he wants. Shelly knows that you are a Crawler. Ron knows that you are a Crawler. And we can guarantee that the customer service representative (rep) that performs your walk will be thoroughly briefed before meeting you for the appointment. The customer service rep will probably schedule a long appointment for you because of your reputation as a Crawler. This is good because he will need the extra time to answer all of your questions. So, let's get into the details of the walk-through appointment, which in your case is an inspection.

Setting the Walk-Through and Closing Date

When your house is within 30 days of completion, Shelly should be asking you to set a walk-through date and a closing date. You will rarely see a closing date in the first week of the month. If on the construction schedule a house is supposed to be finished within the first week of the month, almost all builders will try to move it to the last day of the previous month. The logic is "if it's that close, we can get it done sooner." Remember, the end of a month carries a lot of meaning to the builder, especially if you are approaching a quarter or the end of the fiscal year. If you know that the builder is approaching the end of a quarter, then you also know he will be very motivated to close as many homes as he can at the end of the month. Insiders can use this knowledge to their advantage.

If your house was originally scheduled to be completed in the first week of the month, you should probably expect to get a phone call from Shelly. If she calls you and asks you to close a few days early, then you know that the builder needs another closing for that month. You understand that you might be able to take advantage of this situation and, if you do, you want to express concerns about the house being rushed to get it done. You don't want the builder to hurry and possibly get something wrong. Insiders know that Shelly will say something like, "I assure you that everything will be done and that the builder always keeps quality as a first priority." She might also say, "This is a great benefit for you because now you won't have to pay a full month's interest at the closing." This means that your closing costs will be lower. But because you are an Insider, you know who Shelly is really trying to benefit from the earlier closing—the builder.

Because you have been watching the construction process, you should have a good idea if there is enough time to finish the house a few days early. If you are confident that it can be done, then ask Shelly, "What will the builder give me as compensation for the change in dates?" After all, you have already made your plans to move into the house for the later date. Shelly will offer you something if she needs the closing bad enough. Whatever she does offer, you will ask for something more. You know that Shelly would never give you the whole bag of M&Ms, so ask for more. She may say okay, or she may have to check with her boss. If the builder needs the closing, then they will agree to your terms. Some examples of what you could ask for would be options that are easy to add to your home like appliances; you could ask for a garage door opener or a microwave. Or you could ask for a $1,000 credit toward your closing costs or the option you've already picked. Use common sense and your negotiating skills when asking for your compensation.

Next you want to add something very important to the deal. You want to make sure Shelly understands that the quality in the house is more important than free upgrades or compensation and that you will only consider doing this if your house will be completely done at the closing. If Shelly says something like, "There might be a few things that still need to be done to the house after you move in," then tell her to forget the deal. A few things to a builder could be 100. Insiders do not agree to close on uncompleted homes unless they are getting a giant compensation in return. We have seen such giant compensations in the way of a few thousand dollars in options or even in one case where three months' home mortgage was paid by the builder. Unless you get compensation valuing $2,000 or more, we recommend that you do not close on an incomplete home.

If you do make a deal with the builder for extra options or compensation for moving up your closing date, **you must get it in writing.** Make sure that everything you and the builder agreed to is written in the form of an addendum to the contract. We have seen builders rush to make a deal trying to meet deadlines; when the house closed, they refused to honor it. Builders can get away with this because it was just a verbal agreement. After the buyers close on their homes, they had no leverage to force the builder to comply because they didn't have the agreement in writing.

Unless you are making a deal like the ones described here, you will be given a set date for your walk-through and to sign closing documents. Most agents will try to schedule these two appointments on the same day. Builders want you to go to your walk-through and then immediately sign your closing documents; this way, they control the closing. If it's the end of the month, the builder will be especially adamant about keeping the buyers on schedule to ensure all the documentation is completed for the home to close on time. You see, builders expect you to close no matter how many punch list items you have. Practically everything that can be wrong with your home will be considered a minor repair to the builder.

Insiders consider everything except paint touch-up a major item. You don't want to set your closing appointment on the same day as your walk-through. You want to explain to Shelly that you are not going to close on the home until it is completely done, and you want to schedule the walk-through appointment for two days prior to your closing date. That way, if there are any items on the punch list, they can be corrected before you sign the closing documents. Shelly won't like this at all, but she will have no choice but to schedule you as you request. Remember, you have been preparing Shelly for this day from the beginning, so she should not really be surprised. You want to remind Shelly that you'll be videotaping the walk-through and be sure to say to her, "I need to have my own copy of the checklist during the walk-through." You want this so you will be able to follow each item as you go through the room. This is very important for you, and we'll explain why in the next section.

Insider Tidbit:

Some builders will try to set your appointment to sign the closing documents (docs) before your walk-through (walk). You see, once you sign the docs, the loan is funded, and the house will be recorded in your name; the house has closed. Once you close on your home, you will be completely at the mercy of the builder. What if your walk-through turns up a lot of defects? You'll be stuck with no leverage to get them fixed. No matter what Shelly might say, there is never a good reason to close on your home before you complete the walk-through.

Be aware of the second tactic they use if you question signing the docs before your walk. They will try to assure you that you can delay the funding of the loan until you give permission. This is true, but mistakes happen. We've seen it, and sometimes the loan funds anyway. What would you do then? No amount of reassurance would change an Insider's mind. An Insider would never go to a closing appointment before a complete walk-through of the house.

The Builder's Checklist

A customer service rep will meet you at your new home to do your walk-through. He may be the superintendent, his assistant, or someone who you have never met. You may not know him, but he has certainly heard all about you. We will call your customer service rep "Mike" for simplicity. Mike will introduce himself to you and your Realtor if you are using one. If you do have a Realtor, then you want her there, and she can be the one to film the walk-through for you. Mike will want to be at his best because he is going to be on film. As you know, the videotape will be important in the future to use as proof in case you have any trouble getting things fixed.

At this meeting, Mike will have a checklist to go over during your walk-through; this is the one you asked Shelly for a copy of earlier. Either she or Mike will give you a copy of the list so that you can follow each item as you go through the rooms. This list helps make sure that Mike doesn't skip any items that need to be discussed. We've seen situations where the customer service reps will get behind on their scheduled appointments, so sometimes they will try to rush the walk-through to catch up. Insiders are never rushed; they always look very carefully at each item. If you don't have a copy of this list, how can you be sure that each item is covered? Remember, you are a Crawler who is going to make us proud. So make certain you have your copy and follow along. Ask all the questions you need to, to make sure you know how everything works and where everything is.

At the end of the walk, you will be given a copy of Mike's checklist with both of your signatures on it. He needs a copy to show that he has completed his appointment with you, but this checklist is not the only list that both of you will be signing.

The Punch List

We have talked about the punch list several times, but we want to take a little time here to explain it completely. Builders do not have defect lists or lists of incomplete items because these terms sound very negative. They have punch lists, as if you can just punch these minor items out with very little effort. The punch list is created during your walk-through; it's where Mike will list everything that you both see wrong with the house. But, be aware that Mike won't really be looking that hard for something to put on the punch list. It's pretty much up to you to notice everything. Builders don't want you to be looking for things to add to the list because that means even more work that they have to come back and do. The smaller the list, the less work and the better the builder looks.

You should know by now why builders hate Crawlers, and the walk-through is the chance for you to be the best Crawler in the world. You will have Mike write down everything that is not perfect. Some of the following questions should be on the checklist, but we wanted to give you a feel for what you should prepare for.

Start by looking at the yard and exterior of the houses. Are there any roof shingles missing or problems with the outside? Is the house clean, outside and in? Where do you need paint touch-up, outside and in? You want to look at the floor covering and make sure there are no seams, gouges, or scratches that need repair. You want to look at the railings, light fixtures, light switch plates, and electrical outlet plates. Are they all there and working? Try every door in the house. Are all the doorstops in? Look in the closets and make sure the rods and shelves are present and sturdy.

Try all the plumbing and flush the toilets a couple of times. Are the towel racks, shower doors or rod, and toilet-paper fixtures in place? You want to look at the countertops and the cabinets. Are there any marks, chips, or gouges? Look inside all of the cabinets and drawers. Are any shelves missing? Are the hinges fastened tightly? Try every drawer to see that it moves in and out smoothly. Make sure that all of your appliances are demonstrated fully. You need to look at every handle and part of everything. When you are looking at the light fixtures, make sure that all bulbs are there and try every light. Many times, superintendents will come in and borrow parts from cabinets and/or light fixtures to put in other homes; they do this to complete another home for an earlier closing. It is very easy for the supers to forget to replace the borrowed parts with new ones.

It is very important for you to look at and try everything inside and outside the house. You will list every questionable item on the punch list. Some builders will not come back and repair items if they were not on the punch list. A gouge in your kitchen floor may not be repaired if it is not on your original punch list; the builder could argue that the damage was created when you moved your refrigerator. If you have a crack in a tile on a countertop, it may not be fixed because the builder might argue that you dropped something on it after you moved in. So you must write down everything and get it on videotape; a builder can never argue with videotape. Once you have made your complete punch list, you will sign it and so will Mike. He will give you a copy of the walk-through checklist along with a copy of the punch list. This punch list is what you will be signing off as the repair work is completed.

Reschedule if You Have To

We recommend that you reschedule your walk-through if you have more than 20 items listed on your punch list, not counting locations for paint touch-up. If you have more than 20 items listed, the builder did not take you seriously when you said you expect the house to be complete. If you reach 20 items on the list, you can stop the walk-through and kindly tell Mike that you will need to reschedule because this house is not done. Mike may want to continue, but tell him that you made it very clear to everyone that you will not accept an incomplete home. Tell him that you will reschedule with Shelly when the builder can have the home complete. Also tell him that you are rescheduling the closing date until such time.

If for some reason the builder did not perform before now, this will put him in high gear. In your case, as an Insider you will not be in this position because you have been watching all along; both Shelly and Ron know that you will not be easy to close unless everything is right. We expect your walk-through to go well because you have used the skills you learned from this book; but in some cases you may have to reinforce your Crawler status at the walk-through. Be polite but be firm when talking to Shelly about rescheduling. Tell her how disappointed you are about the walk-through. Make sure she understands that you will be reviewing the videotape and you do not want to have another walk until these items are corrected. Tell her to call you when she has set up another appointment. Now, of course if you do postpone the walk-through, you will have to reschedule your closing appointment, too. Rest assured that Shelly will remember this fact. But, you should remain flexible and polite when resetting these appointments. Remember when we talked about a cushion of time to move? Here is a prime example of when you may want that flexibility. It would assure you a completed home when you do move in.

New-Home Nightmares

We want to share with you a few true nightmare stories of what can happen at a closing. We are doing this to stress how important it is to follow the guidelines. We also want you to understand how much suffering you are going to avoid because you are an Insider.

On one occasion, the superintendent's assistant telephoned Jeff and asked him to come down and be present for a walk-through. Because it was only Jeff's third day in the business of new homes, he was more than eager to come and watch. Little did Jeff know that the assistant had never done a walk-through in his life, and he was hoping that Jeff would do it for him. Of course, Jeff refused and watched as the assistant fumbled through the whole procedure. This particular home was priced at $245,000 with a beautiful pool and waterfall installed in the backyard. Because this home was a previous model, it also had several special features, such as an alarm system, front and backyard landscaping with electronic sprinkler controls, and several upgraded appliances. It was embarrassing to watch this assistant try to cover each item, as he could not answer half of the questions that the homeowner had. Not only did he not understand how to explain and demonstrate the home, but the home had several defects in it as well. The punch list had over 100 items listed as needing repair, some of which would require the subflooring on the second floor to be removed; this was major repair work. This house never should have closed in that condition, but it did.

In another community, by a different builder that Susan worked for, a home that sold for $350,000 had a walk-through where over 150 defects were found in the house. These included missing roof tiles and holes in the exterior walls where coach lights should have been. There were also several missing fixtures in the interior of the home. Even with these defects and omissions, the builder still expected the homeowners to close on their home. The builder tried to claim that these items were minor, and he still considered the home finished. He put on pressure to force the buyers to close on their home before the repairs were even started, and they did.

For our final example, we want you to picture walking into your new home, and just after you pass under the chandelier in the entryway, it comes crashing down to the floor. This happened in one community. Remember the weak ceiling braces we talked about in chapter 9? This was one of those weak braces that some idiot installed and then attached a chandelier. If it had fallen down a few seconds sooner, there could have been serious injuries and a hefty lawsuit filed against the builder. This kind of shoddy construction happens when a builder sacrifices quality in order to meet deadlines. Once again, incredible as it may sound, this house still closed even though it had over 50 defects on the punch list, including repairing the ceiling and replacing the chandelier.

You may think that if you were in any of the situations described here that you would never close on your home before it was truly finished with everything completely repaired. Since you are reading this book, you are right. But, if you weren't reading this book and trusted your builder, you could easily be caught in the Closing Trap, which we will explain completely in the next chapter. We just wanted you to see how important it is to use all of the steps in this book.

Chapter Summary

The walk-through appointment is your chance to inspect everything. The builder wants you to think of this appointment as just an orientation to the features in your home, but Insiders know that this is a serious inspection.

If the builder is approaching the end of a quarter or for any reason needs more closings in a particular month, he may offer you the chance to move up your closing date. If you do this, you must demand that the house will still be 100% complete or get several thousand dollars in compensation for your trouble. Of course, whatever deal you make must be in writing. If it's not, the builder may refuse to honor the deal.

During your walk-through, you are going to make us very proud; you're going to be the best Crawler in the world. Take the time to look at everything and we mean everything. Make certain nothing is missing and try everything to make sure that it works properly. Insiders don't allow impatient customer service reps to rush them. Insiders also take their time and get all their questions answered.

If your punch list gets to be over 20 items, we recommend that you refuse to continue the walk-through. Don't reschedule for another appointment until Shelly assures you that all the items from the partial punch list and everything else in the house has been completed. You must make Shelly understand that you are very disappointed in the condition of the home. She will not be happy about rescheduling, but you are not going to give her a choice. If you were to accept a home with over 20 defects, then you would be falling into the Closing Trap that is set by every builder. Insiders never get caught in the Closing Trap.

Chapter 11

The Closing Trap; Don't Get Caught!

In this chapter:

- Pictures of Closed Homes
- The Builder's Agent
- The Escrow Coordinator
- The Superintendent
- How They Close the Trap
- How You Fight Back
- The Homebuyer's Protection Addendum (HPA)
- Chapter Summary
- Copy of the Homebuyer's Protection Addendum (HPA)

Pictures of Closed Homes

The pictures that you see on the previous pages are of houses that the builders considered complete. The first house had numerous items inside that weren't finished, plus it was supposed to have a landscaped front yard with an automatic sprinkler system installed. This home also passed the city inspection in this condition and was issued a Certificate of Occupancy. As you can see, there is a pile of concrete roof shingles two feet high in the front yard and the sprinkler system has not even been started. The homeowners tried to delay closing until the home was complete by refusing to sign documents for one week, but they told the builder they could not wait any longer to move in. This picture was taken after the second walk-through was conducted. The builder actually had two chances to get it right and failed both times. He obviously had no intention of completing the home before it closed escrow. Unfortunately, these homeowners became victims of the Closing Trap.

The second picture is of another home that not only closed in this condition but closed without a city inspection. The city does not care if the home is closed or not; it is only concerned if the house is occupied prior to its inspection. This homeowner paid her money and closed on her home even though she could not move into her house. She trusted her builder when he told her that the inspection was just a formality and that it would be fine to close before it takes place. She had faith in her builder and ended up with a house that had over 40 defects when it finally did pass inspection several days later. When she was finally allowed to move in, her front yard still needed to be landscaped, including an automatic sprinkler system. Remember how important it is for publicly traded companies to have closing numbers at the end of the month? This house also closed on the last day of the month. It looked terrible and imagine the danger for this homeowner's small children. Wouldn't you love to have your children playing in this front yard with holes, cinder blocks, and bags of half-filled concrete? Sadly, her family became one more victim of the Closing Trap.

We want you to look closely at these pictures. These are real homes with real people living in them. They are not just statistics or numbers, as the building industry would have you believe. The owners were expecting to move into their dream homes, and they were emotionally devastated when they saw their dream homes turn into nightmares.

You may wonder why people would close on homes in this condition. There are several reasons why, and there are several players who take part in the Closing Trap. Suppose you have just finished your walk-through and there are 20 or 30 items on your punch list. The builder will act like it's nothing and expect you to close on your home. Shelly will tell you that it is fine to close because all punch list items will be fixed in a timely manner. So everyone expects you to close on your home. Why? Because both the builder and Shelly want their money; if you don't close on your home, no one gets paid.

Here's the problem. Once the builder has your money, you go to the bottom of the priority list. Think about it. If these punch list items are so easy and can be done so quickly, then why weren't they done before you had your walk-through? If you have been a Crawler from the beginning, you won't face this problem. But to make you the Crawler that would make us proud, you need to fully understand this information. Please read this chapter very carefully. We are going to explain how the Closing Trap works and identify all of the players that cause it to take place.

The Builder's Agent

We are going to start with Shelly so you understand why she wants you to close on a home that is not finished. The builder pays Shelly on a commission basis. She may get paid the day after the home closes, or it may be on a certain payday if she is an employee. In most cases, builder's agents are paid twice a month. Typically, Shelly would be paid on the 15th and the last day of each month. The amount paid on the 15th will be from all the houses that closed between the 15th and the end of the previous month. The amount paid at the end of a month will come from the closings between the 1st and 15th of the current month. If you close on your home on the 30th of the month, Shelly will get paid about two weeks later. If you delay your closing until the 1st, then Shelly won't get paid until the end of that month. She now has to wait 30 days instead of two weeks. If Shelly does not have a lot of closings to rely on, that extra two weeks could make a big difference in her budget. This is one reason Shelly might be motivated to try and convince you to close right after the walk-through. Plus, sometimes builders will pay bonus money to

Shelly if she gets a certain number of homes closed. These bonus bucks can sometimes reach hefty amounts, which again are not paid if the homes don't close when they are expected.

Another motivating factor for Shelly is the builder, himself. The builder does not see you as a human; he sees you as only a number. This number is part of the total amount of closings that will occur during the month. The builder doesn't care if you have 20 or 120 items on your punch list. He only cares if he can get a Certificate of Occupancy so that he can force you to close on your home. The builder will apply pressure on Shelly either directly or through her boss, the vice president of sales. Shelly may feel terrible about the way your house looks at the closing, but it is her job to represent the builder and if she doesn't she may lose her job.

The following true story will give you an example of the pressure that Shelly might receive from the builder. Jeff once had the president of a building company call him and ask why the houses weren't closing. Jeff told him that the houses were in such poor condition that they couldn't pass the city inspection. Jeff went on to tell him that the homeowners couldn't move into their homes without an inspection. The president was furious with Jeff and told him these exact words: "Jeff, just because the homeowners can't move into their homes is no reason not to close escrow." Jeff replied, "But when the homeowners close on their homes, they are paying their money. They actually own the home at that point and they are paying daily interest charges on a home that they cannot even move into." The president again was furious and quickly replied, "Jeff, you need to stop being part of the problem and start being part of the solution. We need to get these homes closed before the end of the month!" With this stern admonishment to Jeff, the president was saying that he did not care how bad the homes were. He only cared about getting them closed, and if Jeff stood in the way he would be fired. This kind of pressure on builder's agents can force them to do many things against their conscience. Shelly could be a wonderful and caring person, but under certain situations if she allowed that caring personality to come out, she could lose her job.

There are other forms of pressure that Shelly will use to get you into the Closing Trap. Shelly might know that your lease is up and that you have to move on a certain day or you'll be without anywhere to live. If you have to be out of your lease on the first of the month, then Shelly knows that you will most likely agree to close on your home even if it has several items on the punch list. You won't have much choice because you have to move and you didn't plan for a cushion of time. Plus, you let Shelly know all of your details. Basically, she knew too much and used that knowledge to pressure you into closing.

You may have just closed on your previous home and your moving truck is loaded up, and it has to be delivered to your new house. If the movers can't deliver your housing goods when scheduled, they must store them on the truck, and this will cost you several hundred dollars. Again, you didn't plan for a cushion of time. So, you decide that it would be better to close on your property instead of getting a hotel room and paying hundreds of dollars for storing your household goods. If these problems don't create enough pressure for you, there are many more to come.

The Escrow Coordinator

If you are buying a home from one of the larger builders in the country, then your contract and subsequent paperwork will be handled by a person known as the escrow coordinator. You may never see this person or talk to her at all, but she is the person who makes sure that your loan has been approved and that nothing has happened to change that status. She also sets up your title appointment so that you can sign documents and close on your home. The escrow coordinator manages the paperwork from your new-home buying process and provides all of the builder's appropriate paperwork to the title company on time to close on your home.

When the vice president of sales or the president of the company wants to know how many closings to expect in any given month, they go to the escrow coordinator to find out. She keeps track of all the sales and closings made company-wide in her office. Many times the escrow coordinator will be the sounding board of an angry president or vice president of sales if the company is not meeting its goals. The pressure for an escrow coordinator to get the homes closed can be intense at certain times of the year.

Because the escrow coordinator is not in direct contact with the homeowners, she is not emotionally involved with them. All she sees are numbers, every day. She is under pressure to get closings and get them done on time. If she is told that a house passes inspection for a Certificate of Occupancy, she expects the house to close soon after and if possible on the next day. It doesn't matter to her if the house looks terrible or not. She just needs to get it closed, and she will apply any pressure that she can on guess whom. That's right, Shelly will be getting pressure from the escrow coordinator to get that home closed.

Builders know what makes people move; besides threatening to fire them, they offer money. So many builders will offer a bonus to escrow coordinators if they can get a certain amount of homes closed within a month. The more homes that close, the bigger bonus she will receive. This incentive obviously adds to the pressure that will eventually be put on Shelly's shoulders. We have seen situations where escrow coordinators go as far as calling the home buyers themselves to pressure them into closing. Sometimes they will offer extra incentives to get them to close if they are nearing the end of a quarter. Unfortunately, they will also use strong-arm tactics and threaten to charge them up to $100.00 a day or more for delaying the close. We will discuss this tactic fully a little later in this chapter. The main point for you to understand is that the escrow coordinator is another person who sees you as only a number and has an enormous amount of pressure to see your closing take place on schedule.

The Superintendent

We have talked about Ron earlier and how he might be paid a bonus if he meets his closing goals. What we didn't say is just how these goals are met. Builders consider houses ready to close when they are issued a Certificate of Occupancy. We have seen houses that were issued this certificate with over 150 items on a punch list. So it's obvious the superintendent is not pressured to completely finish the houses; he is only pressured to get them to pass inspection. As soon as he can get the Certificate of Occupancy, he can tell the escrow coordinator and she will set up the title appointment.

The builder only cares if the house can legally pass inspection in order for it to close. The superintendent has the pressure on his back to get the house to that point. This is why the superintendent wants to finish the house as soon as he can. He wants to get the pressure off of his back. For an extra incentive for the superintendent, he may be paid a bonus if he can get houses to pass inspection on schedule. Maybe he'll get even more money if he gets it done ahead of schedule.

After the Certificate of Occupancy is issued and the escrow coordinator has set the closing appointment to meet her goals, it will be up to Shelly to get you, the buyer, to show up at that appointment. If Shelly can't get you there, then she is considered to be negligent in her job performance. Remember we stressed how important it was for Shelly to establish rapport with you? This is where it becomes most important. Shelly must now convince you to close on your home even if it isn't finished. All of her friendly efforts to get you to like her and trust her will be put to the test and will pay off if she succeeds. Shelly has the escrow coordinator and the builder breathing down her neck, plus she doesn't get paid until you close. All of this pressure is on Shelly, and she had better be able to perform. If she can't get you to close, then the escrow coordinator or her vice-president may have to intervene. If this happens too often, Shelly will lose her job. None of the players who are applying the pressure to Shelly care much about you, the buyer, except for your money. You are simply a number that represents a goal that must be met by the builder.

How They Close the Trap

Okay, you understand how the pressure game is being played, and you know who the players are. And you say, "So what?" You have been in pressure situations before, and you won't give in to pressure. All you have to do is refuse to close, and there is nothing the builder can do to you, right? Wrong! The builder not only plays the pressure game to set up the Closing Trap, but he can use his contract to complete it. In the contract that you signed, there will be a section that read something like this:

> Construction shall be considered to be completed and fully performed when approved by the appropriate city or county department and shall be deemed completed and complying with the terms of this agreement when the appropriate department has issued a Certificate of Occupancy (or like document), permitting occupancy of the property.

What this clause means is that the builder does not have to finish your house in order for him to demand that you close on it. All the builder is required to do is to get a Certificate of Occupancy. You may have over 100 items on your punch list, and he can still legally require you to close on your home. Take another look at the homes at the beginning of this chapter. Both of these homes received a Certificate of Occupancy and were delivered to the buyers in the same condition as when they passed the inspection. We have seen expensive semi-custom homes pass inspection with over 150 defects in the house. Is this what you had in mind when you bought your home? Of course not, but wait, there is more. Remember the other section of the contract that Shelly briefly reviewed? It read something like this:

> If buyer does not fully perform when required, seller has the right to give an extension to the buyer to perform, but the buyer will be required to pay $100 a day to seller for every day of said extension. This amount will be added to the price of the home and will include every day of extension including the day of performance.

Are you starting to get the picture? You have signed an agreement that allows the builder to deliver a house that only requires a Certificate of Occupancy. No matter how many defects are in your house, you must close on the deal or you will be charged $100 a day until you do. We have seen these terms written in every new-home contract that we have used, and sometimes this extension fee is set at a lot more money. These terms are there for only one reason and that is to catch the unsuspecting buyers in the Closing Trap.

The trap starts at the first meeting that you have with Shelly. She establishes rapport with you and gets you to like and respect her. This way she can control you, and when it comes to closing time you won't be a problem. Shelly will know what your living situation is and try to use that to the builder's advantage. Shelly will know if you don't have any place to stay because of a lease or the sale of a home. If Shelly cannot get control over you, then the escrow coordinator will have to step in and try to gain control. She may offer an incentive for you to close on the home, or she may try to get the vice-president of sales to convince you to close. If none of these efforts work, the builder can play hardball and demand that you close or be in default of your contract. If you go into default, the builder can cancel the sale and keep all of your money. The builder can also charge you the agreed-upon fee to extend the closing; this could be $100 a day. Sometimes this fee is added to your closing costs, and sometimes the builder will demand a few days' worth of fees before the extension is granted. We have seen all of these remedies used by builders, and in every situation the homeowner always lost.

How You Fight Back

As an Insider you now know how many people are going to try and pressure you into the Closing Trap. Because you have this knowledge, you have been sending strong signals and warnings from the first day that you are a Crawler. Shelly knew from her first meeting with you that you were going to be a tough customer. When you visited her community, you told her that you would be videotaping the construction process and possibly even having an inspector review your tapes. You were very thorough on all of your questions. You even let it slip that you are very familiar with the state contractor's board and the Better Business Bureau. Shelly also knew that you had no intention of closing on your home unless everything was finished, and she made sure Ron knew about your feelings.

After you made a strong impression with Shelly, you met with Ron and established your reputation as a Crawler with him. Throughout the building process, you reinforced this status with Shelly and Ron so that they would give that extra care to your home. As you watched the construction process, you were able to get any mistakes corrected right away because you had them on videotape. Better yet, you had very little to get corrected because they knew you were watching.

Added to your Crawler status, as an Insider you were able to research the builder in the proper way. You got state contractor's board and Better Business Bureau reports, and several opinions from homeowners. Insiders do not get caught in the Closing Trap because they research a builder completely before they buy a home from them. But that is not enough; Insiders also research the superintendent because they know that the super is ultimately responsible for the quality that goes into a home. By having the construction process go well and hopefully on schedule, you have avoided a great portion of the trap.

Builders can snag buyers in the Closing Trap if they can control the buyers. Buyers get caught by not doing research about the builder and the superintendent. Remember all of those techniques that we have talked about in chapters 6 through 10? If you followed the guidelines, then you won't get caught. Do you understand how important it is for you to use the techniques that we have explained? You want the super to make sure that your house is right. You know he already does a good job from your research, but you want him to give your house a little extra care. With that extra care, your house should be complete at the time of closing.

We believe that a house is not complete until there are no items on the punch list. The building industry, of course, believes that a house is complete when it is issued a Certificate of Occupancy. As we have shown with our pictures and our experiences, these two definitions vary to a great degree. So what would an Insider consider an acceptable walk-through? If your house has 10 items on the punch list or fewer, we would agree to close if most of these items were cosmetic in nature. Cosmetic means paint touch-up, very simple replacements, or minor cleaning. It does not mean missing roof tiles or missing closet doors. It does not mean unfinished flooring or a neglected front yard. Look at the house in the "Introduction" of this book. The builder considered this home complete with the exception of a few minor cosmetic repairs. Would you consider grout work minor? Insiders don't, but builders do. If you have more than 10 items on your walk-through, then do not close on your home.

In chapter 10, we told you to set your closing date two days after the date of your walk-through. You told Shelly that you would not close on the home if there were any items on the walk-through. Because Shelly and Ron have gained great respect for you, they most likely have made sure that your house was completely done. But if you do end up with over 10 items to do, you now have two days to let the builder fix or repair these items before you sign your documents. Shelly will tell you that everything is minor and will be fixed immediately in the hopes to get you to close sooner. You will tell Shelly that you are glad the items are minor and, because they are, there is no reason for the builder not to have them fixed before you sign your closing documents. Shelly will not be happy, but she will put the pressure on Ron to get everything fixed before your title appointment.

Builders design the Closing Trap to catch unsuspecting buyers, but it doesn't work on Insiders; you are far from unsuspecting, and you are not easily manipulated either. Builders want to get the closing done on time, and if they cannot manipulate the buyer to make it happen, sometimes they will bend over a little bit to accomplish it. But sometimes the builder decides to play hardball with you. If you are refusing to sign your docs to close because of the condition of the house and the builder is completely uncooperative, you should threaten to go to the press. You can tell Shelly that you are contacting your local news station and will show them the videotape of your walk-through. You will also tell the news station that the builder is trying to force you to take a house that is not completed. You should ask Shelly if she is willing to appear on camera, or if there is someone else who would represent the builder. You will tell Shelly that you would like to meet her at your house to show the defects that you are unhappy about to the news team.

This is not an idle threat; if your house has several things wrong that are listed on the punch list, then you have a valid complaint. The last thing a builder wants is to get bad publicity on the news stations. Builders spend thousands of dollars every month trying to build a good image, and one negative television report can wipe out a whole year's worth of advertising. Because the builder knows that you are an astute buyer, he will not want to take a chance on a negative television report. To make your threat even more credible, you should call the television station and find out which reporter would handle such a consumer complaint. Most news stations have a staff that investigates consumer complaints; if you live in a city where a lot of new-home building is being done, then it is valuable news to the whole community.

The Homebuyer's Protection Addendum (HPA)

In chapter 6, in No. 15 of the Sales Office Questions, we instructed you to ask Shelly if the builder would accept the Homebuyer's Protection Addendum (HPA). If your builder will accept the HPA, then you cannot get caught in the Closing Trap. You see, when you sign your new-home contract, you can add addendums to it that become a part of the contract. Addendums can be used for clarification, like to describe incentives for buying the house and/or special nonstandard features that you are purchasing in the home. They can also be used to change something that is stated in the contract. The HPA is written for the latter purpose. You do not want to be forced to close on a home just because it has been issued a Certificate of Occupancy, and you do not want to be subject to a daily fine for refusing to close on the builder's scheduled date. The HPA allows you to refuse to close on your home until all punch list items have been completely done. It also gives you the option of closing on the home with the agreement that you will withhold funds from the builder until all punch list items have been complete. If you have the HPA in your new-home contract, you never have to worry about the Closing Trap. There is a copy of the HPA at the end of this chapter so that you may make a copy of it to use in your new home search. We suggest that you make every attempt to get the builder to accept this as a part of your contract.

If the HPA is so wonderful, why isn't it a part of the contract already? Why does everyone have to ask for it? First of all, only Insiders know about the Closing Trap and understand how it works. Second, the HPA is making its début now that the tides are changing in favor of you, the consumer. Third, builders hate the thought of being forced, in writing, to complete your home before they can get it closed. But it sounds perfectly fair for a home buyer to expect the house to be finished before he pays for it, doesn't it? Every builder that you talk to will fight you on this concept. We have not seen one builder who does not try to catch people in their Closing Trap. But this book is about educating people and exposing the builder's secrets, including how he uses the Closing Trap. You are going to be one of the many thousands of our readers who will be part of making a change in how the new-home building industry operates.

When you negotiate your new-home contract, make a strong attempt to get the HPA into the contract. If the builder won't accept it, ask Shelly why he cannot guarantee that your house will be finished before you close escrow. Shelly will not have a good answer for this question. She will tell you that any punch list items will be minor and that her customer service department will see that they get everything fixed in a timely manner. This argument is nonsense. If the items are minor and easily fixed, there is no reason not to have them fixed before you close escrow and move into your new home.

Remember, you will be telling Shelly that you will not be able to set up your closing date until at least two days after your walk-through because you will need all items to be fixed before you move into your new home. If you are able to include the HPA in your contract, you can close on the same day as your walk-through. All that you are asking for Shelly and the builder to do is to guarantee that the house will be completed before you pay him for it. Think about this: Would you pay for a new car if it had a "few items" that still needed to be adjusted or even added? No, no one would. What is so difficult in grasping the concept that you want the same "completeness" in a house before you pay entirely for it, just as you expect in a new car? Surely this concept is not unreasonable to the builder. Shelly will fumble with trying to justify why he cannot guarantee a completed home. She will be frustrated with you at this point because there is simply no valid reason for the builder not to guarantee a completed home. The only reason for a builder not to agree to the HPA is because it keeps them from being able to use the Closing Trap.

If Shelly stands strong and says that she cannot include the HPA in the contract, then use that as a negative in your negotiation. Your best option is to get the HPA included in the contract. If you're determined to buy a house here and since the Builder won't agree to have the home completed in writing, you want something else as compensation. Here is when you could start your negotiations with Shelly. But if you're not that far into the conversation with her, remember to bring this point up when you do negotiate for the house and get something from the builder because he refused the HPA.

It's an extremely important step that you are taking by asking for the HPA. Even if the builder refuses to include it, you will have sent another strong message that you are going to be the most difficult buyer in the world if there is anything wrong with your house at the time of closing. You have already sent firm notice to Shelly that your closing will not take place for two days after your walk-through. Shelly knows that you are definitely a Crawler and that if there can only be one perfect house done on the block, then it must be yours. Insiders command this respect and you are now an Insider. You have learned the techniques that make builders move, and you will use these techniques to ensure that you get a quality, well-built home.

There is a copy of the HPA at the end of this chapter. The spaces to fill in are easy to understand. For the "Buyer" space, you would fill in your name; you are buying the house. The "Builder/Seller" space would be the company from which you are buying your house. The date will be the same as the day you signed the contract for purchasing your house. The "Lot" and "Block Number" spaces correlate to the designation within the community, which lot of what block will your house be built on. The "Community" will be the name of the neighborhood where you are buying your home. There is a blank space in paragraph #5 for the amount to withhold in escrow, if necessary. We recommend that you ask for 5% of the price of the home.

For example, if your home sold for $100,000 then you would want to withhold $5,000. The builder would hate to have this much money withheld and he would be highly motivated to complete your house on time. This is what you want; you never want to be forced to withhold money. You want your house to be perfect on the walk-through, and the HPA provides strong motivation for the builder to make that happen. Finally, you would sign the space for "Buyer signature," fill in the day you sign the HPA, and the builder's designated, legal representative will sign below you in the space for "Seller signature." Shelly, the new-home agent does not sign this form.

There is one final technique to staying out of the Closing Trap, and it is called a *withholding*. You would use this technique if you were not able to have the HPA included in the contract. If your home is in terrible condition and the contract demands that you close, then go ahead and close escrow. However, instruct your lender to withhold a percentage of the funds to pay for the home. This procedure is commonly done when flooring is not installed in the home before the closing. The lender withholds the funds that pay for the floor covering until it is installed and then the funds are released. You can use this same procedure, but in this case you will withhold funds until the builder completes your home. Gauge the percentage you withhold on the amount of work still to be completed. You don't want to withhold so much as to be really devastating to the builder, but you want enough to gain his attention. Just as with the HPA, 5% of the price of the home is a good amount to withhold. The builder will not like it, but there is little he can do. There most likely won't be anything in the contract about withholdings, and you are not refusing to close escrow. You would not be violating any terms of the contract. But, you should review the contract to ensure this is true. This final technique, coupled with talking to the press, if necessary, should motivate even the most difficult builder to perform.

Chapter Summary

In chapters 6 through 10, we explained how to keep out of the Closing Trap. Many of the techniques that you will use in the negotiation and the building process are step-by-step instructions to avoid the Closing Trap. In this chapter, we told you what the Closing Trap is and gave examples of how homeowners get caught. You can now realize how important it is to follow the guidelines throughout the complete buying and building process. If you do, you will never get caught in the Closing Trap.

Before you close on your home, you want no more than 10 items on your walk-through. These items should only be cosmetic in nature such as paint touch-up. Never close with more than 10 items on your walk-through. If the items are easily fixed, then the builder should have no problem getting it done immediately, and then you can close escrow.

If for some reason you have not been the best Crawler in the world and the builder is pushing you into the Closing Trap, you can use the media. Suggest to Shelly that you want a news team to come out and see the unfinished items on your home. You want her to state on camera that the builder is trying to make you close on your home even though it is not finished. Good Crawlers never have to get to this point, but it's a strong ace in the hole if you need it.

If you are able to get the HPA into your contract, then you have the best situation of all. With the HPA, the builder is actually agreeing, in writing, to have your house finished before he gets paid in full. This concept scares builders to death, but Insiders like you think it is fair. If you are able to get the HPA included in your contract, then the builder will make every effort to have your home completely finished before you even do your walk-through. If you do not have the HPA, then you must be the best Crawler in the world because you do not have a contract that forces the builder to finish the home.

The HPA that we include at the end of this chapter is an example that we wrote. You are welcome to use it in its current form, if you like. Remember, you can write any addendum that you choose to add to your contract; of course, you have to get the builder to agree to it. If you decide to change the HPA, make certain you still have the option of withholding a substantial amount of money in escrow. You want to make the builder perform, and there is no better motivation than withholding his profits.

Finally, even if you can't get the HPA into your contract, you can still do a "withholding." You can instruct your lender to withhold funds until you get all of your punch list items fixed. This way, you are not violating your contract because you are still closing escrow, but you still have some of the builder's money and that will motivate him to get your punch list items fixed on a priority basis.

We want to reassure you that you will not be the only one promoting the Homebuyer's Protection Addendum. By the time you read this chapter, you may have seen us on television or heard us on the radio. We will be traveling across the country promoting our book and the HPA. We truly believe that together we can make a difference in the building industry. We really want to see a level playing field between the buyers and builders, and feel the HPA is a giant step in that direction. Please don't hesitate to write and let us know about your success in your new-home experience. We are also very interested in learning about the builders who are willing to accept the HPA. It is our goal to see the HPA widely accepted by all competent builders. We think this would make it much better for future home buyers to have a more enjoyable and easier time in their buying experience.

The Homebuyer's Protection Addendum

Buyer(s)_____and the Builder/Seller
_____agree to make this addendum a legal
part of the purchase agreement signed on Date_____, for
Lot #_____ of Block #_____ at the Community known
as_____.

The Seller and Buyer(s) agree to all of the following conditions:

1. Homebuyers have the right to a quality built new home.
2. Homebuyers have the right to videotape the construction
    process and have this tape reviewed by a private home
    inspector.
3. Homebuyers have the right to expect their home completed
    without defects or any punch list items left unfinished before
    closing escrow. This does not mean simply obtaining a Certifi-
    cate of Occupancy. It means there will be no outstanding items
    left undone from the walk-through inspection of the home.
4. *Punch list* is defined as the original list of defects created
    during the walk-through orientation of the house. The
    Builder may have other terms for this original list of defects
    or items requiring repair, but all terms refer to the same list.
5. If the Buyer agrees to close on their home before all punch
    list items have been completed, then the Seller agrees to al-
    low the Buyer to withhold up to $_____ in escrow until
    all punch list items have been completed and signed off by
    the Buyer. Only after the Escrow Agent has received a copy
    of this signed Builder's form showing all items have been
    completed to the Buyer's satisfaction will the funds be re-
    leased by the Escrow Agent to the Builder/Seller.
6. The Builder agrees to have all punch list items completed
    within 30 days after closing or the Buyer/Homeowner may
    have the items completed and use the funds withheld in es-
    crow to pay for such repairs. After all punch list items have
    been paid for and completed, then the remaining funds will
    be released to the Builder.

Buyer(s) signature_____Date_____

Seller(s) signature_____Date_____

Chapter 12

Finally Moving In— But Just One More Thing

In this chapter:

Whoopee!! It has been a long wait, but you are finally in your new home. You are eager to decorate and arrange everything to make your new home just the way you want it. This is a happy time for you, and it should be. We want to make sure that you are happy for a long time in this home. Because you are now an Insider, we know that your new home will be in great condition, and there will not be any punch list items to be corrected. But we want you to do just two more things.

First, you need to "trip" all the locks in your house with your new house keys. Typically, the construction superintendent has a master key that works on all the locks in the neighborhood. The house keys, your keys, when used in the lock will reset the tumblers and cancel the master key. By tripping the locks this way, you are assuring your privacy and security for your new house.

But don't forget the garage door. It has a lock, too. Second, you need to take a personal walk-through of your house by yourself.

Your Personal Walk-Through

We want you to use your walk-through list and go over every room in the house just once more. You need to use every light socket and plug. Turn on and off every switch and use every option on your appliances. To put it plainly, you need to use everything in your house. You should have done this on your walk-through, but just in case you missed something it is important to get it taken care of immediately. Both Shelly and the builder know that you are a Crawler; a big sigh of relief came over their offices once you closed on your home. But you want the builder to get anything fixed while you are still fresh in his mind. Giving your house a complete once-over in private will give you time to look in every corner, and you will not feel any pressure to hurry the process. If you find any items that were missed on your walk-through, write them down and submit them immediately to the customer service department, or whoever the builder designates as the proper contact. Builders want to get Crawlers taken care of as soon as they can.

Getting Punch List Items Fixed

If you closed on your home and have a punch list of items that need to be fixed, or you discovered some during your private inspection, you will have to schedule repair time with the builder. The superintendent or his assistant may be the one who is doing the repairs; or maybe the customer service department will send someone out. Whoever is responsible should call and make an appointment with you to schedule the work that needs to be done. You or someone you really trust must be there while he is working. Some supers will just ask you for a key, and they will fix the items while you are at work; this is done for their ease of scheduling the repair, and so you will not have to take time off from your busy schedule. We don't recommend doing this because the work is always done better if you are present to watch it.

Plus, you shouldn't trust your super with your house key. Typically, the super is not the one to do the work, it will be his assistant, someone from customer service, or even a worker from a subcontractor. It's likely to be someone you've never met. Do you want your house key floating around with different people that you don't know? Would you leave your house key with the cable or electric company for their workers to have access to your home? Of course not, because you know these workers would be unsupervised. It's the same situation here, and the builder's construction staff can change often. You do not know who is doing your repairs. You really should never let anyone into your home once you have taken possession unless you are present as well. We have seen not only thefts, but also negligent damage done by incompetent and uncaring construction personnel.

It is an inconvenience for you to have to take valuable time from your day to come in and watch a repair being made, but it is essential that you be there. We know how inconvenient it is, and that is why we want you to be a great Crawler in the first place. Good Crawlers don't have to worry about supers or assistants coming back and fixing things because they were motivated to do it right the first time.

Dealing with Subcontractors

You may have items on your punch list that must be fixed by a subcontractor (subs). These items are still the responsibility of the builder to make sure they get done, so don't let him tell you that it's not. The builder is responsible for making sure that the subs do the work and do it right. Less than reputable builders will try to dodge their duty to finish your punch list and/or warranty commitments by claiming that it is the responsibility of the subcontractors. Of course, you won't have this problem because you did your research. But just to let you know how bad it could get, we'll give you an example.

You listed on your punch list, from the walk-through, that there are a couple of drawers that will not close properly in your kitchen. Your super sees you in your car and tells you that the sub that installed the cabinets is supposed to come out and fix the drawers. A person from the builder's customer service department left a message on your telephone, giving you the sub's name and phone number to call him and make an appointment. You try calling, but the sub never answers the phone. You leave a message and give him your number to call you back to set up an appointment. After waiting several days and not getting a call back, you try contacting the customer service department to complain that the sub will not return your calls. The builder's customer service doesn't answer either, so you leave a message for them to call you back about the problem you are having with the sub. Three more days go by, and you hear nothing from anyone. So you try the sub again; no answer, and you leave your telephone number again. You call customer service back and of course you have to leave another message because no one answers the phone there either.

At this point, you are very frustrated, but you also have a life and you get busy and forget to keep calling the builder or the sub. Five days after your last call to the builder, you come home from work to find a message left on your door. It is from the subcontractor who installed the cabinets. It reads something like, "I came by to fix the cabinet drawers but no one was home. Please call my office to schedule another visit." Now you are furious; how could that subcontractor be so stupid? You want to call the builder's customer service and complain but it's after business hours, so you go inside your home and yell at the dog or anyone else who might be present. When you do reach the customer service department the next day, someone actually talks to you and tells you that the sub called them and said he went to your house but no one was home. The customer service representative acts like it was your fault for not being home.

If you think this scenario is far-fetched or unbelievable, then think again. We have seen it happen hundreds of times. Trying to get warranty work done can be the most stressful part of buying a new home, but not for Insiders who do the proper research before they buy. If you somehow do fall into this situation, you must take the following steps to get your work done.

The first thing to do is go to the sales office and complain to Shelly. She may tell you that she can't do anything, but she can. Shelly knows who the supervisors are in customer service and she can also go to her boss. Tell Shelly that you want to speak with the customer service supervisor within 24 hours. You can try to get the direct telephone number of the supervisor, but most likely Shelly will take your number where the supervisor can call you. Inform Shelly that if you don't talk to the supervisor within

24 hours, you will go to the corporate office and see this person face-to-face.

This should be enough to get the supervisor to call you and that in turn will motivate customer service to make sure the subcontractor calls you to set up an appointment. If it doesn't, then you can go to the corporate office and complain until someone sees you. The department heads you can ask to talk to would first be customer service. If that person is unavailable, ask for the construction vice-president. If that person cannot talk to you, ask for the vice president of sales, Shelly's boss. If none of these department heads are available, ask for the president of the company. Builders don't like problems, and they will want to take care of you before you get out of hand. If you did any research at all about your builder and picked a decent one, then surely at this point the builder will make sure that you get satisfaction.

Motivating the Builder

But now let's talk worst case scenarios. Let's say you have a friend who hasn't read this book yet. Let's say his builder turned out to be less than decent, and your friend has tried all our previous suggestions. He even tried to talk to all of the department heads but got no results. The next step he would take is to call his builder's agent and tell her that today he is filing a complaint with the state contractor's board and the Better Business Bureau. He is also going to call the local news station to complain about the poor service given by his builder. He intends to show the reporter the problems and explain how the builder has ignored him. He also plans to bring the news crew to the new-home agent's office so that she can explain why the builder won't honor the warranty policy. No matter how bad a builder is, he will almost always perform at the thought of getting negative publicity on television. Even if he doesn't do something at this stage, the state contractor's board can force him to perform if your friend has a valid complaint.

You would never want to be in the position of having to rely on the state contractor's board or the Better Business Bureau. The whole point of this book is to keep you from getting to this point. We described the previous situation simply to show you how bad it can be if you don't use the steps outlined in this book. You want to motivate the builder before he starts building your house. It can be a hard, long fight to motivate any builder after he has your money; Insiders never get into that position.

A Great Resale Value

Why don't we move on to more pleasant thoughts? Since you have done your research and established yourself as a Crawler, your house is perfect. You have a beautiful home and the inexpressible peace of mind of knowing it was built with quality. Because you negotiated a great deal, you will probably have equity in your home soon after you move in.

You also knew which options would increase resale value, and you included some of them into your home. With your Insider knowledge, you bought a great home for a great price. When the time comes to sell your new home, you can advertise quality, and you can show the videotape to prove it. Wouldn't you feel comfortable about buying a home from someone who took the time to videotape and watch the whole construction process? Surely anyone who put that much care into building his home would also put that much care into maintaining it as well.

Living "Happily Ever After"

Doesn't it feel wonderful? You have a brand new beautiful home, and you can fix it up anyway that you like. Everything in your house works perfectly, and that's the way it should be. The feeling of living in a well-built home is a comfort beyond description. You may have several friends who have told you horror stories about their homes. You will also hear about many frustrated people who can't get their builder to fix defects in their homes. But that won't be you, because you had Insider information and you used it.

You will enjoy your home for as long as you live there, and you know that you will get a great price for it when you decide to move. You have joined our list of happy homeowners. We are very excited for you, and we hope that you will take the time to contact us and share your story. You may have ideas that can help other homeowners, and if you would share them with us, we will share them with everyone. You can e-mail us or send us a written letter. Or we would love to see you in person. We do new-home workshops in many cities across the country, and we would love to have you stop by. We have taken a long journey together, and it has required a lot of effort on your part, but doesn't it feel good now? We were happy to be there with you, and we wish you the best of luck in all that you do.

Chapter Summary

In this last chapter of our journey, we told you to trip all your locks to ensure your security and privacy. Also, you need to look at and use everything in your house one more time. Try everything out to make sure that it all works perfectly. If anything does need to be repaired, you want to get it done while you are still fresh in the builder's mind.

We relayed an example of how hard it can be to get a builder to perform after he has your money. If you don't do your research and become a Crawler, you could be in for the most frustrating experience of your life. If you choose the wrong builder, you might even end up with a home that has such serious construction problems that they cannot be fixed. If you choose an okay builder but don't maintain your Crawler status, you could end up with headaches from the attempts to get all the repairs completed. You don't want to be the one telling a new-home horror story, so we relayed several steps to take if necessary to get the builder to perform and repair your house. After all is said and done, you want to be the one who has no problems and is living "happily ever after."

Knowing that you got a great price and a quality built home provides a sense of satisfaction and comfort. You will enjoy your new home, and it will be the dream home that it is supposed to be. Also, you know that you will get a great resale price when you decide to sell. These are the feelings that you should have when you move into your new home, and we are glad that we could help you attain this happiness. Please tell your friends about your experience and our book, so they too can enjoy Insider status and the comfort of a well-built, quality home. As you go forward in your life, may God bless you in all that you do.

The Last Word

Well, how does it feel, now that you are an Insider? We bet you're feeling on top of the world, eager to go out and find your dream home and to get it for a great price. Maybe you know of a friend or maybe someone in your family that you think could really benefit from reading *The Ultimate New-Home Buying Guide*. Why keep the Insider information a secret? Encourage your friend or relative to pick up a copy at their local bookstore.

Or they can order a book directly from the publisher. The total cost is $19.45. It's the cost of the book ($15.95), plus the shipping and handling costs ($3.50). They can order on the Internet at *www.MapleLeafPress.com*. They can call toll-free at (800) 247-6553 and place an order. They can also order by mail, sending a check or money order to:

> BookMasters, Inc.
> P.O. Box 388
> Ashland, OH 44805

If they choose to mail their order in, the check should be written to "BookMasters." Please write the book title *"The Ultimate New-Home Buying Guide"* and "ISBN-0-9706737-0-1," on the check in the memo section. These help to ensure they get the correct book sent to them. Please allow about 2 to 3 weeks to receive the book.

We truly hope to hear how you succeeded in finding and building your dream home. We are looking forward to hearing from you. You can reach us by e-mail at *authors@MapleLeaf-Press.com* or by traditional mail at:

> Jeff & Susan Treganowan
> C/O Maple Leaf Press
> P.O. Box 5002-115
> North Conway, NH 03860-5002

Happy home buying and living "happily ever after!"

Glossary

2 × 4 construction Exterior walls are approximately 4 inches deep.

2 × 6 construction Exterior walls are approximately 6 inches deep.

2-10 warranties A third-party insured warranty purchased by the builder from an insurance company. The builder is responsible for covering repairs during the first 2 years. The remaining 8 years are covered by the third-party insurer.

16 on center (16 O.C.) Width between wall studs. "Sixteen on center" means the studs are 16 inches from the center of one stud to the center of another stud.

Acreage The amount of land area a property has, expressed in acres. One acre equals 43,560 square feet.

Addendum Any additional terms that are put in writing and added to the original purchase agreement.

Adjustable rate mortgage (ARM) A type of mortgage in which the interest rate is keyed to a certain economic index and is adjusted as the index rises and falls. If you have this type of mortgage, your monthly payment could go up or down, depending on the prevailing rates.

Agent A person authorized to work on another's behalf—for instance, a person authorized to sell or buy a house on your behalf. (*see* Builder's agent; New-home agent)

Allowances Sums of money that are "rebated" back to you to purchase various items such as light fixtures. A $500 allowance would allow you to purchase up to $500 worth of fixtures. Additional fixtures would be paid out of your own pocket.

Amortization The process of paying off the loan balance. As you make payments, a certain amount is applied to the principal and a

207

certain amount to the interest. The schedule or table of amortization shows the declining balance as you make payments.

Anchor bolt Required in many areas with seismic activity, the bolt is set in the concrete foundation and connects to the walls of the home. The goal is to prevent the home from moving or swaying in an earthquake.

Annual percentage rates(APR) The true rate of interest for a loan. This rate will include the costs of any points paid, mortgage insurance, and other costs.

Appraisal An estimate of the value of a certain property by a qualified, independent individual.

Arbitration Third-party dispute resolution method in which an arbitrator sits down with both sides, listens to their arguments, and renders a decision (this decision could be binding or nonbinding.) It is used in some disputes to try to avoid legal action. The American Arbitration Association and the National Association of Conciliators are examples of organizations that offer dispute resolution.

Assumption A type of purchase in which the buyer assumes the responsibility of making payments on the seller's home.

Back fill Dirt used to fill in around the foundation after the foundation walls are poured or constructed.

Back-end A ratio used by lenders to determine a borrower's ability to pay. The back-end ratio is the monthly total of a borrower's bills to include the house payment, divided by the total monthly income of the borrower.

Balloon mortgage A type of mortgage in which the loan amount is amortized over the full length of the loan (usually 30 years), but the loan actually comes due after a few years (usually 5 or 7). The first payments go mostly toward interest. The balance of the loan is due in one final installment, called the *balloon payment*.

Basis Your home's value for tax purposes.

Blueprints Detailed plan that is used to construct a home. Also known as *designs* or *plans*.

Broker An agent that is authorized to open and run his or her own agency. All real estate offices and builders have one principal broker.

Builder A person or a company whose business is constructing new homes.

Builder's agent A real estate agent employed by a builder to sell his homes exclusively. (*see* New-home agent)

Builder-grade materials Typically the least expensive, lowest quality materials the builder sets as the standard material for a home.

Building codes Series of state and local laws that set a minimum standard for building practices.

Buy-down A type of financing in which a developer or seller arranges for the buyer to get a loan at a rate below the current market rate. The developer or seller pays interest costs in order to lower the interest rate, but usually raises the price of the house to recoup this loss.

Buyer's agent An agent hired by the buyer to help the buyer find a home and negotiate the purchase of a home. This agent works for the best interests of the buyer, not the seller. Also known as *buyer's broker.*

Cap A limit on an adjustable rate mortgage. Depending on the ARM, the loan may have a cap on how much the interest rate can increase, for instance.

CC&Rs (Covenants, Conditions & Restrictions) Regulations and ordinances that must be obeyed by homeowners.

Certificate of Occupancy A certificate issued by a city or county building inspector to a builder. This certificate allows the home to be legally occupied.

Closing The process of finalizing all the dealings associated with the sale and purchase of a home. Also called *settlement.* This is the time that you sign all the closing documentations (docs) and there is the final exchange of money for the title to the home.

Closing fees Fees charged by the title company and lender to process the closing documents.

Closing trap The unethical practice that home builders use to force home buyers into their homes before they are finished.

Commission The fee an agent earns for the sale of a home, usually a percentage of the selling price.

Commitment letter A formal offer of a loan by a lender. The letter will state the terms under which it has agreed to the loan.

Comprehensive The most expensive type of homeowner's insurance; covers the most potential damages.

Condominium A form of home ownership in which the owner owns the airspace within the walls, but doesn't own the actual walls, ceilings, or floors of his home; the owner may also own a percentage of the common areas, such as the swimming pool.

Contingency A provision included in a sales contract that states certain events that must occur or conditions that must be met before the contract is valid.

Contract The written agreement between the builder and home buyer that states the terms of the new-home purchase (*see* purchase agreement)

Conventional mortgage A type of mortgage made by banks and other lending institutions.

Counteroffer A subsequent offer that makes a change to the original offer. Can be made by either the seller or the buyer.

Crawler A new-home buyer who is very meticulous about everything. He or she presents a visual image of someone crawling under cabinets to see if anything was missed.

Credit report A report of all your debt information compiled by an independent agency. The credit report shows all outstanding debt as well as a record of payment on outstanding debts.

Cul-de-sac A street that dead-ends into a large circle.

Curb appeal How attractive a home looks from the curb or street.

Custom home A home designed by an architect that meets the buyer's needs. Everything in the home is chosen by the buyer.

Deed The legal document that conveys the title to a property.

Default To fail to make payments on a loan.

Depreciation Due to age or obsolescence, the decrease in a property's value over time.

Design center One central office that many new-home builders use to sell options to their buyers.

Docs Abbreviated term for *closing documents.*

Down payment The money you pay up front for the purchase of the home

Drywall A sheet of gypsum sandwiched between two sheets of paper. Used to cover studs and create walls. Also known as *sheetrock.*

Dual agent A real estate broker who claims to represent both the seller and the buyer in a real estate transaction. Some dual agents represent neither the seller nor the buyer—they simply provide general advice and help with the transaction. Also referred to as a *facilitator* or *mediator.*

Earnest money A deposit you make when you make an offer on a house.

Easement A right given by the landowner to use the property. For example, you may have easements on your property for phone lines, utility poles, and so on.

Elevations Exterior view of a home design.

Equity The financial interest or cash value of your home, minus the current loan balance and any costs incurred in selling the home.

Errors and omissions insurance Special insurance for builders and architects to cover mistakes in the home design or construction.

Escrow A trust account created by a neutral third party to hold money for the seller or buyer. For example, when you put down a deposit on a house, it should be put into an escrow account. When the sale is complete, the money can be released from this account to the seller.

Escrow agent A neutral party who holds earnest and deposit money in an escrow account. The escrow agent or office will also perform the closing and title transfer of a new home.

Excavation Removal of dirt and trees at a home site in preparation for the foundation.

Fannie Mae The Federal National Mortgage Association, a private company that both buys and sells mortgages from lenders.

FHA mortgage FHA stands for *Federal Housing Authority*. The government guarantees FHA loans. You can put down a smaller down payment on an FHA loan, but you will also be required to pay mortgage insurance.

FICO scores The scores reported by the **F**air **I**ssac **Co**mpany that are included with your credit report. Lenders use these scores to determine a borrower's ability to pay at a certain point of time.

Fixed-rate mortgage A type of mortgage in which the interest rate is fixed for the life of the loan.

Fizz-bo See FSBO.

Floor-plans Plans of a home given to new-home buyers at new-home communities.

Footings Structural element at the base of foundations, piers, or columns used to support the home.

Foreclosure The legal process in which a mortgage property is seized because of default and then sold.

Frame-walk An inspection of a new home right after the plumbing and electrical work is done. The superintendent and home buyer must be present.

Freddie Mac A private company that buys and sells mortgages from lenders.

Front-end A ratio used by lenders to determine a borrower's ability to pay. The front-end ratio is determined by dividing the total house payment by the total monthly income of the borrower.

FSBO For-Sale-By-Owner; pronounced "fizz-bo." A home that is offered for sale without the use of an agent.

Gag rule Contract provision that prohibits your ability to hang signs outside your home complaining about the builder. Many gag rules also prohibit picketing the builder's offices or model homes as well.

General contractor Builder who is in charge of project and hires all subcontractors and materials' suppliers.

Gift letter A letter that is required if you receive a down payment from any individual as a gift.

Good-faith estimate Lenders are required by law to provide an estimate of all closing costs and escrows within 3 days of your application.

Hazard insurance Insurance that covers the home against damage by such hazards as fire, hail, wind, and so on. The perils covered vary by policy.

Home warranty A guarantee for certain features of a new home—for instance, the materials and workmanship, the main components of the house, and so on.

Homebuyer's Protection Addendum (HPA) An addendum that allows the home buyer to withhold funds at a closing if the house is not completely done. An essential tool to keep out of the Closing Trap.

Homeowner's association (HOA) An association of homeowners who are responsible for enforcing the CC&Rs and the HOA rules in a new-home community.

Housing ratio The percentage of your housing payment (principal, interest, taxes, and insurance) to your monthly gross income. Lenders will use this ratio to qualify you for a loan. Sometimes this ratio is called the *front ratio*. A common ratio is 28%.

Impact fees Taxes imposed by local communities on new homes to fund schools, parks, etc.

Implied Warranty of Habitability Established by the courts, this doctrine states that all new homes are assumed to be suitable for habitation, to be built in a workmanlike manner, and to meet all building codes.

Impounds Amounts of money collected by a lender to pay for insurance and real estate taxes on your property.

Index An economic indicator that is used in setting the rate for adjustable rate mortgages.

Insider A person who has new-home knowledge not available to the general public.

Inspection A close and thorough examination of a house and property. A licensed individual usually does the inspection.

Interest rate The percentage the lender charges you for borrowing money.

Joint tenancy An equal, undivided ownership in a property by two or more individuals.

Joists Small beams placed parallel on top of the sills. Supported by columns or piers, the joists in turn form the support for the subfloor.

Junk fees Extra fees charged by lenders to increase their profits on new-home loans.

Lien A claim against a property.

Limited warranty Any warranty that has specific exclusions and conditions.

Listing agent An agent who obtains the listing from the seller/builder and lists the home in the multiple listing service (MLS). This agent is working for and owes loyalty to the builder/seller.

Load-bearing wall Structural element of a home that is carrying a substantial weight. Without it, the home would collapse.

Loan officer The person in charge of taking a loan application for a new home.

Loan origination fee A fee charged by the lenders, usually 1% of the loan amount.

Lock in To guarantee a certain interest rate for a certain period of time.

Low-doc loan Mortgage loan that requires little documentation of income and asset levels.

LTV (Loan-to-value ratio) Used by lenders to state how much you have financed. If you put down 20% on a purchase, you finance 80% and have an 80% LTV.

Maintenance fee A fee charged by condominium associations, co-ops, or other homeowner's associations for the upkeep of the property.

Master-planned community A community that is planned before construction that may include schools, parks, stores, and several other amenities.

Mechanic's lien Encumbrance placed against a property to satisfy any unpaid invoices to a subcontractor or supplier.

Model home A home that is used to display a certain model or floor plan in a new home community.

Mortgagee A legal document that pledges your property as security for a loan.

Mortgage banker A company that originates mortgages and then sells them to a secondary market.

Mortgage broker An intermediary between the borrowers and lenders used to find a loan. The broker takes the loan and then packages it for the lender.

Mortgage insurance premium (MIP) The up-front insurance premium you must pay if you get an FHA loan. The insurance helps cover the costs of reselling your home if you default on the loan.

Mortgagee The lender.

Mortgagor The borrower.

Multiple listing service (MLS) A computerized listing of all the homes for sale in an area. Agents are granted access to this service and can use it to find a house in a particular price range or area.

Municipal housing inspector Employed by a city or county, this person inspects construction sites to determine whether builders are adhering to local building codes.

Negative amortization A type of loan situation that occurs when the monthly payments do not cover the principal or interest. Rather than declining, the balance on the loan will actually increase.

New-home agent A real estate agent who works directly for a builder. (*see* Builder's agent)

No-doc loan Mortgage loans that require no documentation of income. Granted only in cases of large down payments.

Nonstandard request A custom change request that is not on the builder's option list.

Options A list of changes of upgrades that a buyer can request in a new home.

Origination fee A fee that covers the lender's cost of making a loan. Typically is 1% of the value of the loan amount.

Overall debt ratio The percentage of your overall debt (housing payments plus any other long-term debt) to your monthly gross income. Lenders will use this ratio to see whether you qualify for a loan. This ratio is sometimes called the *back-end ratio*. A common ratio would be 36%.

Permanent loan Typically a 30-year mortgage loan. (*see* Fixed-rate loan)

PITI Principal, interest, taxes, and insurance—the total monthly payment you make on a house.

Point One percent of a loan amount. Lenders charge points in exchange for lowering the interest rate.

Preapproval letter Letter from a lender indicating that a buyer can qualify for a certain size mortgage at a specified rate.

Preapproved Meeting with a lender and providing all the financial details to get preapproved for a loan. When you are preapproved, you have a definite commitment from a lender. Compare this to *prequalify.*

Prequalify Meeting or talking with a lender informally, providing the lender with your financial information, then having the lender qualify you for a loan for a certain amount. When you are prequalified, the lender gives you an estimate, but does not formally commit to giving you a loan. Compare this to *preapproved.*

Principal The amount of money borrowed and still owed on a loan.

Private mortgage insurance (PMI) Insurance that protects lenders in case of a loan default. Required on almost all loans except the VA loan.

Production home Mass-produced homes built in a development by one builder. Buyers usually have limited ability to customize this type of home.

Proration The division of certain fees. For example, if the sellers have paid for taxes 6 months in advance, they may want a portion of that payment back for the months you are living in the house.

Punch list List of items that require repair or correction. Prepared before closing, usually at the walk-through.

Purchase agreement The written agreement between a new-home buyer and the builder that determines the terms of sale (*see* Contract)

Qualifying ratio The percentages that a lender will compare to see whether you qualify for a loan. (*see* Overall debt ratio; Housing ratio)

R-value How resistant a material is to air infiltration, providing an insulation value.

Realtor Real estate agent who is a member of the National Association of Realtors (NAR).

Recording fees Charges at the time of closing to record legal documents with the county.

Resale value The appraised value of a home on a certain date.

RESPA (Real Estate Settlement Procedures Act) This act requires the lender to disclose certain information about a loan, including the estimated closing costs and APR.

Rough-in Installation of various mechanical systems such as plumbing, electrical, heating, etc. After these are roughed in, you perform your frame-walk. (*see* Frame-walk)

Salability Features in a home that make it easier to sell but do not increase the value.

Sales contract The contract you draw up when you want to make an offer on a home. Sometimes called the *purchase agreement.*

Seller carryback Financing arrangement in which the seller loans the purchaser money to purchase the property. The seller "carries" an amount due to purchase the property in the form of a loan. Also known as *seller take back.*

Self disclosure A form required by most states in which the seller must disclose any known defects of the home.

Selling agent *See* listing agent.

Semi-custom home Type of home where the buyer can make several changes to the design, except for exterior and load-bearing walls.

Setback The minimum distance between a lot line and the location of structures, buildings or streets.

Sills Wood that sits atop the foundation walls.

Single-family home A separate unattached home on its own land.

Slab-on-grade foundation Foundation that is built directly over dirt with no basement or crawlspace.

Soils test Test to determine subsoil conditions that impact on the foundation's design.

Spec (speculation) home Home that is built without a buyer with the speculation of selling the home before it is completed.

SPECS (specifications) Brand names, types of materials, and installation methods to be used in a new home's construction.

Standard features Features that are included in a new home at no extra charge.

Standing inventory A new home that is completely built and has not sold.

Stucco Exterior finish of a home made from wet plaster or concrete.

Studs These are the 2×4s and 2×6s that make up the skeleton of your home.

Subagent The agent who works with you to purchase a house, but is paid by the seller. Also known as *cooperating agent*. Compare with *buyer's agent*.

Subcontractor (subs) Independent companies or workers who are hired by the builder to perform various construction tasks on the home.

Subdivision A piece of land divided into several plots on which homes are built.

Subfloor Plywood sheathing that sits atop the joists.

Superintendent (super) The person who is responsible to coordinate the construction of a new home. The super oversees all of the subs and makes sure that the work is done correctly.

Survey An examination of the property boundaries to find out the quantity of land, location of improvements, and other information. Usually, the surveyor creates a map or drawing of the legal boundaries of the property. (Or: Measurement to determine the exact boundary lines of a property.)

Tap fees Charges by utility companies to hook up new homes.

Term The length of a loan.

Title Ownership of a piece of real property.

Title appointment The appointment that is made for you to close on your home. (*see* closing)

Title company Company that issues title insurance and participates in the closing of property transactions.

Title insurance Insurance that protects the lender and buyer against any losses incurred from disputes over the title of a property.

Title search The process of reviewing court and other records to ensure that there are not liens or claims against the property you are buying.

Topo-board The map of a new-home community showing which phases are under construction. These maps are usually displayed in the center of the model home sales office.

Townhouse A home that is attached by at least one wall. Similar to a condo but often has a little more yard or a garage.

Tract home See Production home.

Trusses Prefabricated roof system.

Underwriting The process of evaluating a loan to determine whether the loan is a good risk.

VA loan A type of loan for veterans, guaranteed by the Department of Veteran's Affairs. No private mortgage insurance is required with this loan.

Walk-through (walk) The final inspection conducted by a new-home buyer before he closes on his home.

Zero-lot-line homes Homes that are built right on the property line with no setbacks required.

Zoning Laws that restricts the use of property to defined applications.

Index